Killer Mom

Darlie Routier

Brenda Irish Heintzelman

pg. 1 KILLER MOM – DARLIE ROUTIER IS AN OPINION-ESSAY ONLY AND IS NOT MEANT TO SERVE AS ANY MEDICAL, LEGAL, OR PSYCHOLOGICAL ADVICE.

copyright@2018 Butterfly Publishing, Traverse City, MI

All rights reserved. No copies, reprints, or electronic transmission of any part of this essay without written permission from the author who can be reached at missmensa@gmail.com.

Killer Mom ~ Darlie Routier is an opinion essay written to explore the case of convicted child murderer Darlie Routier. This essay is not intended to serve as any medical, legal, or psychological advice in any way, shape, form, or fashion.

Introduction

On June 6, 1996, Darlie Routier dialed 911 and reported that an intruder had just stabbed her and two of her children, Devon and Damon, who were sleeping on the floor of the main floor family room within just a few feet of their mother.

According to Darlie, while she was sleeping, an intruder fatally stabbed her children then proceeded to slash her throat and stab her on the arm. And she slept through it all. Well, that's her story anyway. And for more than twenty-two years straight she's been sticking to it.

She said that Damon, age five, ran over to her and tapped her on the shoulder saying, "Mommy, Mommy" and that's what finally woke her up.

Yes, she slept through having her throat slashed but she woke up when her young son tapped her on the shoulder. Her 5-year-old son, by the way, who was far too injured to be able to walk or to talk.

She said that when she opened her eyes she saw a man "standing" at her feet "walking away from her".

Darlie says she followed the man, quietly walking behind him, with Damon supposedly walking behind her, as the intruder made his way through the house headed toward the garage. Evidently the intruder wasn't in any big hurry. And evidently Darlie never gave it a thought to scream for her gun-toting husband, Darin, who was sleeping in the second-floor master bedroom. The couple's youngest child, baby Drake, was safely tucked in his crib upstairs near his father.

Darlie, Darin, and baby Drake, weren't the only ones who slept through it all. The family dog, Domain, a known barker, also slept right through the massacre along with the family's overweight psycho-cat who they kept in a cage next to the sofa that Darlie claims she was sleeping on in the family room.

So, the intruder took his sweet time walking out of the residence while Darlie walked behind him. And then when Darlie saw that the intruder had dropped a bloody butcher knife on the floor of the utility room on his way to the garage, she stopped following him and picked up the knife.

She set the knife on the counter. She looked around and saw that both Devon and Damon were bleeding. And suddenly, she realized that the intruder had stabbed her children.

That's when she suddenly decided to scream.

"DARIN!!! DARIN!!! DARIN!!!"

Darin came rushing down the stairs and saw his sons laying on the floor covered in blood. Right away he raced over to Devon to begin performing CPR. However, with his first attempt to breathe into his son's body, blood spurted from the little boy's chest.

Darlie ran to the kitchen and grabbed the phone to call for help. She would later claim that she also grabbed towels and laid them on her younger son's back, for what purpose that served nobody knows, while she was on the phone with the police dispatcher.

Darin's stories are just as unbelievable as Darlie's stories are. This might help explain why they both failed their lie-detector tests.

Because they are both lying.

One of Darin's stories goes that he was sound asleep upstairs and suddenly he woke up to the sound of a wine glass breaking on the floor in the kitchen. He describes the sound as a "soft swoosh-like" noise that caused him to spring to his feet and run down those stairs to see what was going on.

That's one of his stories anyway.

Another one of his stories is that he was sound asleep upstairs when he suddenly heard Darlie scream out his name three times in a row.

And another one of his stories is that he was sound asleep upstairs when he suddenly heard Darlie scream out the name of their oldest son three times in a row. "Devon!!! Devon!!! Devon!!!"

He seems to like telling his story to make it sound as if he spent a lot of time trying to save Devon's life by giving him CPR. There's just one little problem with his claim. He said that the first time he blew air into Devon's mouth that blood went all over and landed on his face and in his hair. So that would mean that he spent a whopping five seconds administering CPR to his oldest son.

It sounds like Darin didn't go anywhere near little Damon. And neither did Darlie, though remember she did claim that at some point she laid towels on his back.

Neither Darin or Darlie held their children in their arms or comforted them as both boys lay on the floor of the family room bleeding to death.

Instead, Darlie was busy hanging on the phone for six minutes straight talking about her jewelry and the butcher knife.,

"I already picked it up! We could have gotten prints maybe!".

It's unclear what Darin was up to when Darlie was first on the phone with the police dispatcher. Perhaps he was outside planting the bloody sock out in the yard.

Darin was an avid gun toter. And according to their story, an intruder had just walked toward the garage INSIDE THEIR HOUSE after FATALLY STABBING TWO OF THEIR CHILDREN!

Yet, neither Darin or Darlie ever mention that Darin ever got his gun and searched the house for the intruder or even just stood there armed and ready in case the intruder entered the family room again.

So, it's unclear what Darin was up to when Darlie was on the phone with the police dispatcher for over three minutes until the first responding police officer entered the house.

Then at one point in the call, after the police officer was already standing right there in front of them, Darin can be heard on the 911 tape saying something to Darlie that evidently made her very angry. Based on her angry reaction to Darin, it sounds like he had just accused her of killing their kids.

Darin would later say that he wasn't sure if he was dressed when he ran down the stairs or if he even had his glasses on. He doesn't know if he ran back upstairs to get dressed or to get his glasses.

But he knows that he didn't wash the blood off.

Yet, when the first officer arrived at the Routier home just three minutes after Darin supposedly came racing down those stairs, Darin didn't have blood on his face or in his hair.

And he was dressed.

And he had his glasses on.

And it appeared he was attempting to give CPR to one of his sons. The same son who Darin claimed he was not able to give CPR to because in his first breath, blood spurted from the boy's chest cavity.

Remember, Darin was a gun owner, a very proud gun owner, who wasn't shy at all about showing off his 1911 to total strangers. Yet, when he supposedly heard his wife's blood curdling screams, he didn't think to grab his gun just in case he needed it to protect his family.

pg. 6 KILLER MOM – DARLIE ROUTIER IS AN OPINION ESSAY ONLY AND IS NOT MEANT TO SERVE AS ANY MEDICAL, LEGAL, OR PSYCHOLOGICAL ADVICE.

The Routier home had a great security system complete with outside lights that turned on by automatic sensors. But for some odd reason on this night the security system wasn't turned on. And the outside lights never turned on either which is very strange considering the "intruder" would have been entering and exiting the home directly in the path of the sensors.

So, let's recap – Darlie slept through it all. Darin and the baby and even the family dog and the psycho-cat slept through it all too.

The outdoor lights never turned on.

The intruder killed two innocent children but left the adult alive, the person who would be able to identify him to the police.

The intruder decided to leave the murder weapon behind.

The intruder walked. He didn't run.

He took his sweet time making his way back out of the house even though he knew that the adult he had just attacked was still very much alive and able to identify him was walking right behind him.

There were no cars speeding out of the neighborhood when the police officers arrived within three minutes of the moment that Darlie claims the intruder was sauntering toward the garage.

The proud gun-owner Darin didn't grab his gun before he ran down the stairs. He carried the gun on him during the day. So, it was obviously within reach and a normal part of his routine. Yet, at the moment he hears his wife screaming downstairs he never gave the gun a second thought.

Nothing at all was stolen from the home so it wasn't a burglary.

It was a double-homicide.

Of two small children.

Which, of course, makes absolutely no sense at all.

And finally, most telling, is that Darlie's injuries were called "superficial" and were determined to be consistent with being "self-inflicted", while Devon and Damon's injuring were deep fatal stab wounds to their vital organs.

I think I know the reason why Darlie and Darin's stories make no sense. Because I think that Darlie killed her children and I think Darin knew it from the moment he first heard his sons screaming out for him to help them.

In May of 2016, I received a phone call from Darlie's best friend. Well, she used to be Darlie's best friend, until she was called to testify for the prosecution at Darlie's trial. She said that Darlie wasn't acting normal and she begged both Darin and Darlie for her to get some help.

But Darlie didn't want to go get any help, according to her friend, because she was concerned how that would look down the road in a custody battle.

And ever since her best friend testified at her trial, the family has refused to acknowledge her existence.

When she called me in 2016, she told me that when she saw Darlie at the hospital, that Darlie confessed to her, face to face, that she killed her children. And I was also told that Darin had threatened the woman who called me that she better keep her mouth shut.

When I asked her why she didn't say so at the time she said she was afraid. She said Darin had guns.

That being said, I'm not so sure that she didn't tell the prosecutors what she knew. There's a point during her trial testimony where they very clearly instruct her to not say what the judge had already told her she couldn't say. So, I don't know if the information may have, for some unknown reason, been kept from open court for the jurors to hear.

Whether or not the court knew it back then, they know it now. Because I told them what I was told.

Because, in my opinion, the woman who called me was telling the truth.

In my opinion, this is what really happened the morning of June 6, 1996 at the home of Darlie and Darin Routier.

The day before the murders, Darlie had a lot of rage going on while her children appeared to be doing their best to avoid her. Devon stayed at his friend's house all day then called around dinnertime and begged to be able to spend the night. Darlie said no. Little Damon spent his afternoon riding his bike around the neighborhood – alone. The boys were just five and six years old.

Her best friend's mother spent the day at the Routier home doing the laundry. She said that Darlie was angry all afternoon and was slamming doors and stomping around and SHARPENING HER KITCHEN KNIVES. When her daughter picked her up at the end of the day she said that she was worried that someone was going to get hurt. And just eight hours later poor little Devon and Damon Routier were dead.

I think the reason Darlie was so enraged that afternoon is because she learned that Darin and her kid sister, Dana, (another "D") skipped out of work for the day and spent the afternoon together doing who knows what, who knows where, for really who knows how long. Dana was staying with the Routiers at night and working with Darin during the day.

Then suddenly that evening Dana had to leave after nine p.m. supposedly because her boyfriend wasn't answering his phone and she "didn't want him to be worrying about her". I think Dana had to suddenly leave that evening because Darlie ordered her and her husband both out of her house.

I think when Darin finally dared to head back to the house that he and Darlie continued to fight.

I think the only reason the boys were sleeping on the floor of the family room was because their parents were too busy fighting to notice their children watching TV long after what would have been their bedtimes.

If they had bedtimes, that is.

Darlie claims, of course, that she and the children were watching television together. Except there's just one little problem with her claim. She has zero recollection of what TV show or movie she and her children were supposedly watching. If a mother's children are brutally murdered just hours later, then surely she would remember what show they were watching. Not Darlie. She doesn't have a clue.

I think Darlie and Darin were fighting the night away and then finally at 1:00 a.m. Darin walked up those stairs to go to bed without his wife.

That's another issue with their changing stories – Darin says he went up to bed at 11:00 p.m. but Darlie says he went upstairs at 1:00 a.m.

I think when he walked up those stairs he laughed at Darlie's request for a divorce and told her he was taking the house, and the children, and that she'd be lucky to ever see them again.

And I think Darlie responded by threatening to kill them first before ever allowing Darin to have custody of them.

Its called spousal revenge filicide. And I think that's exactly what Darlie's motive was when she murdered her boys.

And then just ninety minutes later, at 2:31 a.m., Darlie dialed 911 to report that an intruder had stabbed her and two of her children.

Darlie's supporters claim that you can tell by her 911 call that she is a frantic mother trying to get help for her children.

But she isn't.

She is a KILLER MOM who was trying to make sure that her intruder story made it onto the taped line.

~

911 TRANSCRIPT

Recorded by The Rowlett Police Department

pg. 11 KILLER MOM – DARLIE ROUTIER IS AN OPINION ESSAY ONLY AND IS NOT MEANT TO SERVE AS ANY MEDICAL, LEGAL, OR PSYCHOLOGICAL ADVICE.

June 6, 1996.

00:00:00 911 Operator – Rowlett 911. What is your emergency?

00:01:19 Darlie Routier – Somebody came in here. They broke in.

00:03:27 911 Operator – Mam?

00:05:11 Darlie Routier – They just stabbed me and my children.

00:07:16 911 Operator – What?

00:08:05 Darlie Routier - They just stabbed me and my kids. My little boys.

00:09:24 911 Operator – Who did?

00:11:12 Darlie Routier – my little boy is dying.

00:13:07 911 Operator – Hang on. Hang on. Hang on.

00:15:03 Darlie Routier – Hurry.

00:18:11 Darlie Routier – Mam.

00:18:19 911 Operator – Hang on Mam.

00:21:26 Darlie Routier – Mam.

00:23:00 911 Operator - Unknown medical emergency… 5801 Eagle Drive.

00:26:24 Darlie Routier – Mam.

00:27:12 911 Operator – Mam. I'm trying to get an ambulance to you. Hang on a minute.

00:28:20 RADIO - (siren)

00:29:13 Darlie Routier – Oh my God. My babies are dying.

pg. 12 KILLER MOM – DARLIE ROUTIER IS AN OPINION ESSAY ONLY AND IS NOT MEANT TO SERVE AS ANY MEDICAL, LEGAL, OR PSYCHOLOGICAL ADVICE.

00:31:09 911 Operator - What's going on Mam?

00:32:13 Darlie Routier – Oh my God.

00:35:20 Darlie Routier - Thought he was dead. Oh my God.

00:39:29 Darlie Routier - I don't even know.

00:43:15 Darlie Routier - I don't even know.

00:49:28 Darlie Routier – He was breathing.

00:51:15 Darlie Routier - Are they still laying there?

00:55:06 Darlie Routier ...oh my God ...what do we do...

00:57:17 911 Operator #1 ...time out 2:32...

00:58:26 Darlie Routier ...oh my God...

00:58:28 911 Operator #1 ...stamp me a card Clint...

01:01:02 911 Operator #1 ...80...

01:01:16 RADIO ...(unintelligible)...

01:02:13 Darlie Routier ...oh my God...

01:03:05 RADIO ...(unintelligible)...

01:04:07 911 Operator #1 ...need units going towards 5801 Eagle Drive ...5801 Eagle Drive

01:04:07 Darlie Routier ...oh my God ...my baby's dead...

01:07:08 Darlie Routier ...Damon ...hold on honey...

01:08:11 Darin Routier ...(unintelligible)...

01:08:22 911 Operator #1 ...hysterical female on the phone...

01:10:03 Darlie Routier ...(unintelligible)...

pg. 13 KILLER MOM – DARLIE ROUTIER IS AN OPINION ESSAY ONLY AND IS NOT MEANT TO SERVE AS ANY MEDICAL, LEGAL, OR PSYCHOLOGICAL ADVICE.

01:10:10 Darin Routier ...(unintelligible)...

01:10:26 911 Operator #1 ...says her child has been stabbed

01:11:28 Darlie Routier ...I saw them Darin...

01:12:21 Darin Routier ...oh my God ...(unintelligible) ...came in here...

01:14:10 911 Operator #1 ...ma'am ...I need you to calm down and talk to me...

01:14:24 RADIO ...(unintelligible)...

01:16:25 Darlie Routier ...ok...

01:16:26 SOUND ...(unintelligible)...

01:17:12 911 Operator #1 ...twice Clint...

01:18:26 Darlie Routier ...didn't you get my address...

01:20:19 911 Operator #1 ...5801 Eagle...

01:22:00 Darlie Routier ...yes ...we need help...

01:22:03 RADIO ...(unintelligible) will be enroute code...

01:24:20 Darlie Routier ...Darin ...I don't know who it was...

01:24:23 911 Operator #1 ...2:33 code...

01:26:15 Darlie Routier ...we got to find out who it was...

01:27:12 911 Operator #1 ...ma'am...

01:28:04 911 Operator #1 ...ma'am listen ...listen to me...

01:29:27 Darlie Routier ...yes ...yes ...(unintelligible)...

01:30:23 RADIO ...(unintelligible) I'm clear ...do you need anything...

01:32:08 Darin Routier ...(unintelligible)...

pg. 14 KILLER MOM – DARLIE ROUTIER IS AN OPINION ESSAY ONLY AND IS NOT MEANT TO SERVE AS ANY MEDICAL, LEGAL, OR PSYCHOLOGICAL ADVICE.

01:32:20 Darlie Routier ...oh my God...

01:34:00 911 Operator #1 ...(unintelligible)...

01:34:22 911 Operator #1 ...do you take the radio Clint...

01:35:23 911 Operator #2 ...yes...

01:36:12 Darlie Routier ...oh my God...

01:36:25 911 Operator #1 ...I...ma'am...

01:38:03 Darlie Routier ...yes...

01:38:17 911 Operator #1 ...I need you to ...

01:38:23 RADIO ...(unintelligible) start that way (unintelligible)... will revise...

01:39:28 911 Operator #1 ...I need you to talk to me...

01:41:21 Darlie Routier ...what ...what ...what...

01:44:25 RADIO ...(unintelligible)...

01:44:28 Darlie Routier ...my babies are dead (unintelligible)...

01:46:20 RADIO ...go ahead and start that way ...siren code 4 ...advise...

01:47:10 Darlie Routier ...(unintelligible)...

01:48:03 Darlie Routier ...(unintelligible) do you want honey ...hold on (unintelligible)...

01:49:17 911 Operator #1 ...ma'am ...I can't understand you...

01:50:21 Darlie Routier ...yes...

01:51:18 911 Operator #1 ...you're going to have to slow down ...calm down ...and talk to me...

01:52:19 Darlie Routier ...I'm talking to my babies ...they're dying...

pg. 15 KILLER MOM – DARLIE ROUTIER IS AN OPINION ESSAY ONLY AND IS NOT MEANT TO SERVE AS ANY MEDICAL, LEGAL, OR PSYCHOLOGICAL ADVICE.

01:55:03 911 Operator #1 ...what is going on...

01:56:29 Darlie Routier ...somebody came in while I was sleeping ...me and my little boys were sleeping downstairs...

02:02:00 RADIO ...(unintelligible) I'll be clear...

02:02:20 Darlie Routier ...some man ...came in ...stabbed my babies ...stabbed me ...I woke up ...I was fighting ...he ran out through the garage ...threw the knife down ...my babies are dying ...they're dead ...oh my God...

02:14:23 911 Operator #1 ...ok ...stay on the phone with me...

02:16:11 Darin Routier ...(unintelligible)...

02:17:06 Darlie Routier ...oh my God...

02:17:29 911 Operator #1 ...what happened (unintelligible) dispatch 901...

02:20:15 Darlie Routier ...hold on honey ...hold on...

02:22:01 911 Operator #1 ...(unintelligible) who was on (unintelligible)...

02:22:26 911 Operator #2 ...it was (unintelligible) the white phone...

02:23:08 Darlie Routier ...hold on...

02:25:26 911 Operator #2 ...they were wondering when we need to dispatch ...so I sent a double team...

02:25:28 Darlie Routier ...oh my God ...oh my God...

02:28:08 911 Operator #1 ...ok ...thanks...

02:28:21 Darlie Routier ...oh my God...

02:29:20 SOUND ...(unintelligible)...

02:30:01 Darlie Routier ...oh my God...

pg. 16 KILLER MOM – DARLIE ROUTIER IS AN OPINION ESSAY ONLY AND IS NOT MEANT TO SERVE AS ANY MEDICAL, LEGAL, OR PSYCHOLOGICAL ADVICE.

02:30:20 911 Operator #1 ...ma'am...

02:31:06 RADIO ...(unintelligible)...

02:31:14 911 Operator #1 ...who's there with you...

02:32:15 Darlie Routier ...Karen ...(unintelligible)...

02:33:15 911 Operator #1 ...ma'am...

02:34:06 Darlie Routier ...what...

02:38:11 911 Operator #1 ...is there anybody in the house ...besides you and your children...

02:38:11 Darlie Routier ...no ...my husband he just ran downstairs ...he's helping me ...but they're dying ...oh my God ...they're dead...

02:43:24 911 Operator #1 ...ok ...ok ...how many little boys ...is it two boys...

02:46:06 Darin Routier ...(unintelligible)...

02:46:25 Darlie Routier ...there's two of 'em ...there's two...

02:48:18 RADIO ...what's the cross street on that address on Eagle...

02:50:15 Darlie Routier ...oh my God ...who would do this...

02:53:13 911 Operator #1 ...(unintelligible) listen to me ...calm down ...(unintelligible)...

02:53:21 Darlie Routier ...I feel really bad ...I think I'm dying...

02:55:06 RADIO ...228...

02:56:06 911 Operator #1 ...go ahead...

02:58:12 RADIO ...(unintelligible) address again (unintelligible)...

02:59:12 RADIO ...(unintelligible)...

pg. 17 KILLER MOM – DARLIE ROUTIER IS AN OPINION ESSAY ONLY AND IS NOT MEANT TO SERVE AS ANY MEDICAL, LEGAL, OR PSYCHOLOGICAL ADVICE.

02:59:22 Darlie Routier ...when are they going to be here...

03:00:22 911 Operator #1 ...5801 Eagle Drive ...5801 Eagle Drive...

03:03:28 Darlie Routier ...when are they going to be here...

03:03:29 911 Operator #1 ...going to be a stabbing...

03:05:20 Darlie Routier ...when are they going to be here...

03:06:20 911 Operator #1 ...ma'am ...they're on their way...

03:08:00 RADIO ...(unintelligible)...

03:08:08 Darlie Routier ...I gotta just sit here forever ...oh my God...

03:11:14 911 Operator #1 ...2:35...

03:12:05 Darie Routier ...who would do this ...who would do this...

03:13:09 Darin Routier ...(unintelligible)...

03:14:26 911 Operator #1 ...(sounds of typing on computer keyboard)...

03:16:08 911 Operator #1 ...ma'am ...how old are your boys...

03:18:20 Darin Routier ...what...

03:19:03 911 Operator #1 ...how old are your boys...

03:20:04 RADIO ...(unintelligible)...

03:20:21 911 Operator #1 ...no...

03:21:01 Darlie Routier ...seven and five...

03:22:17 911 Operator #1 ...ok...

03:23:08 Darlie Routier ...oh my God ...oh my God ...oh ...he's dead...

03:29:02 911 Operator #1 ...calm down ...can you...

03:29:03 Darlie Routier ...oh God ...Devon no ...oh my God...

pg. 18 KILLER MOM – DARLIE ROUTIER IS AN OPINION ESSAY ONLY AND IS NOT MEANT TO SERVE AS ANY MEDICAL, LEGAL, OR PSYCHOLOGICAL ADVICE.

03:30:27 SOUND ...(dog barking)...

03:35:02 911 Operator #1 ...is your name Darlie...

03:36:11 Darlie Routier ...yes...

03:36:26 911 Operator #1 ...this is her...

03:37:09 911 Operator #1 ...is your husband's name Darin...

03:38:22 Darlie Routier ...yes ...please hurry ...God they're taking forever...

03:41:20 911 Operator #1 ...there's nobody in your house ...there was ...was...

03:44:05 911 Operator #1 ...you don't know who did this...

03:45:19 Police Officer ...look for a rag...

03:46:11 Darlie Routier ...they killed our babies...

03:48:03 Police Officer ...lay down ...ok ...just sit down ...(unintelligible)

03:51:11 911 Operator #1 ...(sounds of typing on computer keyboard)...

03:52:13 Darlie Routier ...no ...he ran out ...uh ...they ran out in the garage ...I was sleeping...

03:54:09 911 Operator #1 ...(unintelligible)...

03:56:19 Darlie Routier ...my babies over here already cut ...can I (unintelligible)...

03:59:29 Darin Routier ...(unintelligible) phone is right there...

04:01:28 Darlie Routier ...(unintelligible)...

04:03:01 RADIO ...(unintelligible)...

04:05:02 Darlie Routier ...ya'll look out in the garage ...look out in the garage ...they left a knife laying on...

pg. 19 KILLER MOM – DARLIE ROUTIER IS AN OPINION ESSAY ONLY AND IS NOT MEANT TO SERVE AS ANY MEDICAL, LEGAL, OR PSYCHOLOGICAL ADVICE.

04:08:21 RADIO ...(unintelligible)...

04:09:19 911 Operator #1 ...there's a knife ...don't touch anything...

04:11:18 Darlie Routier ...I already touched it and picked it up...

04:12:05 RADIO ...10-4...

04:15:20 911 Operator #1 ...who's out there ...is anybody out there...

04:16:07 Police Officer ...(unintelligible)...

04:17:06 Darlie Routier ...I don't know ...I was sleeping...

04:18:14 911 Operator #1 ...ok ma'am ...listen ...there's a police officer at your front door ...is your front door unlocked...

04:22:11 RADIO ...(unintelligible)...

04:22:15 Darlie Routier ...yes ma'am ...but where's the ambulance...

04:24:21 911 Operator #1 ...ok...

04:24:23 Darlie Routier ...they're barely breathing...

04:26:17 Darlie Routier ...if they don't get it here they're gonna be dead ...my God they're (unintelligible) ...hurry ...please hurry...

04:31:13 911 Operator #1 ...ok ...they're ...they're...

04:32:18 Police Officer ...what about you...

04:33:06 911 Operator #1 ...is 82 out on Eagle...

04:34:18 Darlie Routier ...huh...

04:35:12 Darin Routier ...they took (unintelligible) ...they ran (unintelligible)...

04:36:28 911 Operator #2 ...(unintelligible)...

04:37:08 Darlie Routier ...we're at Eagle ...5801 Eagle ...my God and hurry...

04:41:03 RADIO ...(unintelligible)...

04:41:22 911 Operator #1 ...82 ...are you out...

04:42:25 Police Officer ...nothing's gone Mrs. Routier...

04:44:10 Darlie Routier ...oh my God ...oh my God ...why would they do this...

04:48:03 RADIO ...(unintelligible) to advise (unintelligible) 200...

04:50:18 Police Officer ...(unintelligible) the problem Mrs. Routier...

04:50:21 911 Operator #1 ...what'd he say...

04:51:29 Darlie Routier ...why would they do this...

04:53:08 Darlie Routier ...I'm (unintelligible)...

04:54:07 911 Operator #1 ...ok ...listen ma'am ...need to ...need to let the officers in the front door ...ok...

04:59:11 Darlie Routier ...what...

05:00:04 911 Operator #1 ...ma'am..

05:00:22 Darlie Routier ...what ...what...

05:01:15 911 Operator #1 ...need to let the police officers in the front door...

05:04:21 Darlie Routier ...(unintelligible) his knife was lying over there and I already picked it up...

05:08:19 911 Operator #1 ...ok ...it's alright ...it's ok...

05:09:20 Darlie Routier ...God ...I bet if we could have gotten the prints maybe ...maybe...

05:13:18 Police Officer ...(unintelligible)...

05:14:18 RADIO ...82 ...we'll be (unintelligible)...

05:17:12 Darlie Routier ...ok ...it'll be...

05:18:08 911 Operator #1 ...ma'am ...hang on ...hang on a second...

05:19:09 Darlie Routier ...**somebody who did it intentionally walked in here and did it Darin!**

05:20:19 911 Operator #1 ...82 ...10-9...

05:21:23 RADIO ...(unintelligible)...

05:22:28 911 Operator #1 ...received...

05:23:05 Darlie Routier ...it's not because.

05:24:12 911 Operator #1 ...ok ma'am...

05:25:13 Darlie Routier ...it's not because.

05:26:20 RADIO ...(unintelligible)...

05:28:00 Darlie Routier ...it's not because.

05:29:08 Police Officer ...(unintelligible)...

05:29:23 RADIO ...received...

05:31:19 RADIO ...(unintelligible)...

05:33:25 911 Operator #1 ...ma'am ...is the police officer there...

05:35:14 Darlie Routier ...yes (unintelligible)...

05:35:23 911 Operator #1 ...ok ...go talk to him ...ok...

05:38:03 RADIO ...(unintelligible)...

Total length of tape is 5:44:28

Courtesy of www.darlieroutierforum.com

Analysis of the 911 Call

As a 911 Operator and Police Dispatcher for five years, I learned a lot about helping people who needed emergency fire, police, or medical help.

Not everybody handled every situation the same way. Some cried throughout the entire call. Some remained calm then broke down as soon as help arrived. Some callers started the call off screaming. Some started the call off hyperventilating or struggling to be able to speak.

Not Darlie. She spoke clearly. She talked about the knife and whether there would be fingerprints on it. And she talked about whether her jewelry was stolen.

Darlie's first statement on the 911 call

Take another look at Darlie's first statement on the 911 call. "Somebody came in here. They broke in".

It appears from her first statement that her priority was not to get help for her children. Instead, it appears her first priority was to be to get her story on a taped line.

Darlie didn't say HELP, MY CHIDLREN HAVE BEEN STABBED. THEY NEED AN AMBULANCE NOW! MY ADDRESS IS 5801 EAGLE DRIVE!

Instead, she wanted the police to believe her story that somebody had broken into her home.

pg. 23 KILLER MOM – DARLIE ROUTIER IS AN OPINION ESSAY ONLY AND IS NOT MEANT TO SERVE AS ANY MEDICAL, LEGAL, OR PSYCHOLOGICAL ADVICE.

At this point the police dispatcher was probably wondering if Darlie had just returned home and found that while she was gone someone had broken into her home.

Callers start off their calls for help by stating their immediate need and by clearly stating their location. In my experience, by the time I was finished saying "Michigan State Police - Heintzelman" the callers were already screaming out what help they needed and exactly where the help was needed.

Remember the murders of Devon and Damon Routier occurred in 1996. Today we assume that the police departments know exactly where we are calling from. But in 1996 "caller ID" was still a relatively new concept. The caller ID monitor was a separate purchase from the phone, and the caller ID package was an additional fee beyond the cost of the phone line.

In Darlie's first sentence when she called for help, she did not report that it was a medical emergency, that she needed an ambulance, or that her children were stabbed. And Darlie did not give the police dispatcher her location.

Instead, she wanted the police dispatcher to know that it wasn't her who stabbed her children. She was laying the groundwork for what was yet to come. She was "fixing blame fast".

"Somebody came in here. They broke in". Even given the story that Darlie expected the police to believe – that an intruder had just stabbed her children – her very first sentence should have been "HELP, MY CHILDREN HAVE BEEN STABBED, MY ADDRESS IS 5801 EAGLE DRIVE IN ROWLETT".

Darlie's use of the words Dead, Dying, and Killed

As a 911 Operator and Police Dispatcher for five years, I learned that parents of dying children refuse to accept the fact that their child is dying, or dead.

Not Darlie.

The words "dying" or "dead" flew out of Darlie's mouth eleven times in her 911 call. In fact, specific to her younger son who was still alive when the first officer arrived, Darlie was saying he was dying or dead even before he had actually died.

This is not normal. This is a person who probably believed her children were dead before she dialed 911.

Long before she dialed 911.

Darlie also used the word killed, as in past tense, her children were already killed. Again, this is not normal for a parent to react to a child's death by readily accepting the fact they were gone. Parents beg EMTs and emergency room staff to try again, to save their child, to do everything they can to save their child's life. Parents sometimes need to be taken away from the child's body so EMTs can do their best to save them.

Not Darlie.

She wasn't anywhere near her dying children. She was busy on the phone with the police dispatcher informing her that her children were dead.

The Barking Dog

Notice the dog started to bark about three and a half minutes after Darlie dialed the phone. That was when the police officer entered the home. The dog wasn't barking at all before the police officer entered the home.

pg. 25 KILLER MOM – DARLIE ROUTIER IS AN OPINION ESSAY ONLY AND IS NOT MEANT TO SERVE AS ANY MEDICAL, LEGAL, OR PSYCHOLOGICAL ADVICE.

Darlie would later tell the police investigators that the dog started to bark as soon as other people entered the home.

But wait. Darlie claimed there was an intruder. She claimed the intruder had just walked out through the garage right before she dialed 911. And the dog was not barking. At all.

He didn't bark at all before the first responding officer entered the house because there was no intruder. And the 911 tape proves it.

It's not because

I am perhaps the only person who believes that Darlie says the phrase "It's not because" three times in a row during her 911 call. I've asked many people to listen to it and nobody ever agrees with me that Darlie says "It's not because" in her 911 call. They think she says a variety of other statements, none of which make any sense specific to the incident.

"It's not because" does make sense. During the phone call it appears that Darlie's husband has said something offensive to her, as if he has blamed her for murdering their children.

She responds by changing her tone in a flash of anger when she says, "Somebody came in here and intentionally did this Darin!".

Darlie is clearly angry when she says makes that statement on the taped line. Surely it appears she has accidently flown off-script to tell her husband off. And then as fast as she flipped from trying to sound as if she was a mother wanting help for her children, to an angry wife whose husband had just accused her of killing their children, she flipped right back from her angry tone to the voice of a mother who didn't understand why it was taking so long for help to arrive.

pg. 26 KILLER MOM – DARLIE ROUTIER IS AN OPINION ESSAY ONLY AND IS NOT MEANT TO SERVE AS ANY MEDICAL, LEGAL, OR PSYCHOLOGICAL ADVICE.

Darlie's refusal to get off the phone

Help had already arrived. The first responding officer entered the home roughly three minutes after Darlie dialed 911. He told her to get off the phone. He told her to help her children. And she refused. She kept hanging on the line saying – "Ma'am? Ma'am? Ma'am?" – to the police dispatcher.

After the police officer had already entered the home, Darlie said to the police dispatcher – "God, please hurry, they're taking forever". And over one minute AFTER the police officer had already entered the home, Darlie FINALLY gave her address to the police dispatcher.

Obviously, since the police officer was already in the house, Darlie knew the dispatcher did not need her address.

In June of 2018, ABC released a four-part miniseries on the case. It was slanted of course, just like MaM was one-sided too. Evidently, changing the facts helps both ABC and NETLFLIX increase viewership. In the ABC miniseries on the case, the officer is portrayed as not having been effective, trained, or professional, and the inference was made that it was because of the first responding officer that the children did not receive emergency medical care soon enough to save them.

In fact, the reason there was any delay at all in allowing the EMTs to enter the home was because Darlie was lying to the dispatcher from the moment she dialed 911. And she was lying to the police officer from the moment he first walked in the door.

Darlie claimed there was an intruder who had just walked out toward the garage just three minutes earlier, right before she dialed 911, so the officer needed to secure the scene before he allowed the EMTs to enter.

Darlie and Darin have both acted as if the police officer did not do a good job when he entered the home.

Well, they're both lying.

In fact, the police officer deserves an award for his reaction to what he found when he entered the Routier home in June of 1996. And any delay in emergency medical help for Devon and Damon Routier lies solely on the shoulders of their parents.

Darlie knew there was no intruder. And my hunch is that by the time Darlie dialed 911 that Darin knew it too. If I'm wrong and he didn't know it beforehand then it certainly appears obvious by Darlie's angry outburst to Darin while she was on the phone with the police dispatcher that he figured it out right then and there that his wife was a murderer.

Darlie's Story

Two minutes into the 911 call, Darlie was suddenly on a roll. "Some man ...came in ...stabbed my babies ...stabbed me ...I woke up ...I was fighting ...he ran out through the garage ...threw the knife down ...my babies are dying ...they're dead ...oh my God...".

"I was fighting". Darlie said she was fighting the intruder. Yet, in her written police statement given just two days later, Darlie said that when her son touched her on the shoulder that she opened her eyes and saw a man "standing at (her) feet, walking away from (her)."

Which is it? Was she fighting off an intruder? Or did she react to seeing an intruder in her house by walking behind him as she would later claim?

Overall, Darlie's 911 call points to her guilt. It also points to a husband who knew right then and there that his wife had murdered their children. "It's not because" stated three times in a row by Darlie on her 911 call clearly shows that she was trying to tell her husband the children weren't killed because of something she had said to him earlier.

While they were fighting.

Before her husband walked up the stairs at 1:00 in the morning.

While his wife chose once again to sleep on the sofa downstairs.

Darlie's Written Police Statement

Darlie had just witnessed her children dying two days before she was writing out this statement at the police department. The funeral was scheduled for the following day. Her mother-in-law, Sarilda Routier had taken care of all the preparations for the funeral while the doctors allowed Darlie to stay in the hospital even though her injuries did not require a hospital stay. The doctors said they allowed her to stay in the hospital to help protect her from the reporters who were waiting to interview her.

So, while Darlie was staying the hospital receiving friends and family members, her children's bodies were being autopsied and then released to the funeral home to prepare them for their burial.

Darlie did not choose the casket they would share or pick out the clothes they would wear. She left that all up to her mother-in-law to handle for her.

The police wanted to interview Darlie. So, they told her that as soon as possible they wanted her and Darin to come to the police department to speak with the detectives and to give a written statement.

On June 8th, two days after the murders, Darlie decided to leave the hospital late in the afternoon. Her children were going to be buried the next day. There was a visitation at the funeral home scheduled for that evening.

Did she leave the hospital early in the day, so she would have time to go to the police station and tell them everything she knew so they could find the monster who murdered her children?

No.

Finally, late in the afternoon when Darlie decided to leave the hospital, the police officers gave her and Darin a ride to the station and offered then to drive them to the funeral home too.

Let that sink in.

According to her story, there was an intruder who broke into her home and murdered two of her children. She knew the police officers wanted to interview her at length and for her to provide a written statement to assist in the investigation.

And she finally made herself available just a couple of hours before she was due to receive visitors at the funeral home for her children's "viewing".

She spoke with the police officers then wrote out a lengthy statement by hand. She and her husband would be two hours late for their son's scheduled visitation at the funeral home that evening, a fact they would later immaturely claim was the fault of the police investigators.

Statement of Darlie Routier

Taken at Rowlett P.D., June 8, 1996

"Darin and Dana my sister came home from working at the shop."

Whoa, now wait just a minute. Her very first sentence in her written statement after two of her children were brutally murdered by an "intruder" who broke into her home is to say that her husband and her sister "came home from working at the shop"???

Seriously?

I think that without realizing what she's done, she has brought right out into the open exactly who she blames for her children's murders. I think that she was so angry that her husband and her sister left the shop together that afternoon, and still were not home after what would have been quitting time, that she and her husband argued until 1:00 a.m. when he went to bed without her. And I think while they were arguing he told her he was through, and that he wanted a divorce, and would be fighting for custody of their children.

And I think that Darlie committed spousal revenge filicide.

I also think that based on her teenage sister's age at the time, that she threatened to report her husband to the police if he refused to help her cover up what she did.

"The boys were playing with the neighborhood kids outside".

Remember this is her written statement about what happened the night that her children were brutally murdered. And remember this statement was written just two days after their deaths.

"The boys..."

She says, "the boys" instead of giving her children's names.

She also says that the boys were playing outside with the kids from the neighborhood. What she doesn't say is that she was routinely overheard by the neighbors to yell at her older children to "get the hell" out of HER house!

In fact, six-year-old Devon had spent the entire day at a friend's house while five-year-old Damon entertained himself all afternoon in the hot Texas sun by riding his bike around the neighborhood. Devon called home at dinnertime and begged Darlie to let him stay overnight at his friend's house. Darlie told him no. According to the woman who called me in May of 2016, when she went to the Routier home to pick up her mother, little Devon came inside the house, hugged her tight, and asked her to take him home with her.

Darlie said no. Could it be that both boys were just like the elderly woman who begged her daughter to leave right away as soon as she arrived to pick her up? Could it be that people in Darlie's life, including her five and six-year-old children knew how to stay out of her way?

"I was finishing up dinner. Damon came home and Devon called and I told him to be home soon because we were going to eat. Darin played with the baby (Drake) with Dana while I pulled everything together to eat. Devon came home and we all ate dinner together."

In truth, Darlie fed Devon and Damon each a bowl of chicken noodle soup which they ate while sitting at a table separate from their parents.

"After we ate we cleaned all the plates."

Dinner consisted of chicken noodle soup.

> *"I was changing Drake while Darin put everything in some containers for leftovers."*

The portrait Darlie is attempting to paint is that they were just one big happy family while she was "pulling everything together to eat". In fact, when her friend arrived after quitting time to pick up her mother who had spent the day doing laundry for Darlie, the husband and sister were still not home.

They waited around, concerned about leaving the boys alone with their mother who they realized was in an incredibly foul mood. After waiting a half hour or so they finally decided to leave even though Darin and Darlie's teenage sister were still not home.

As they drove out of the neighborhood they saw Darin and Darlie's sister driving toward the house. Both had big smiles on their faces and waved to the two women who, in their native Polish tongue, were sharing their concerns that "someone was going to get hurt".

> *"We all talked a little about how happy we were that the shop had been so busy for the past three weeks and that we hoped it would continue since work had been slow for a couple of months."*

Well, if the shop had truly been "so busy for the past three weeks" then it's interesting her husband and kid sister could find the time to leave work for the afternoon.

"...work had been slow" is an understatement. The business was in serious trouble and evidently had been in serious trouble for a very long time. When Darin left his previous employer, he took a few clients right with him, along with his co-worker who at the time was Darlie's best friend. And one by one he lost the clients he had taken from his previous employer.

From the start, Darin did not invest any of his earnings back into the company, as his one employee tried numerous times to convince him he should be doing.

After the murders, Darin insisted there was no financial issue in their marriage. However, the shop rent was already many months past due. He owed back taxes to the tune of ten thousand dollars from the year before. They were late on their house payments. His car was broken down and instead of getting it fixed he drove Darlie's car, leaving her stranded at home.

They were behind on the charge card payments and the accounts were max'd out. Darlie was affectionately known as "Shop 'til she drops Darlie". However, with less money in the bank to even pay one month's worth of bills on the home-front, and with no access to a car to even drive herself to the mall, Darlie was stuck at home and miserable.

It was June, yet their boat was not at the lake because, like Darin's car, the boat was also in need of repairs.

And the couple had two major vacations planned too. How they ever planned on paying for them is anybody's guess. They were set to leave the following week to take an extended family vacation to Darlie's home-town, Altoona, Pennsylvania. And when they returned from their planned two-week vacation to PA, Darlie had a solo vacation planned without her husband and children to Cancun, Mexico.

Remember, they were late on their house payment, the shop rent, the credit card payment, and their back taxes. Her husband's business was failing. To add insult to injury, less than one week before the murders, Darin was turned down by their bank for a five-thousand-dollar loan. He would later claim that the loan was so he could buy a used truck for Darlie's kid sister.

> "Devon and Damon asked if they could play with one of their friends a little longer so we said ok. Darin Dana, and I just sat around and watched a little TV. Later, I'm not sure of exact time I asked Darin to drive Dana (my sister) home because I wasn't feeling to (sic) well. While Darin was gone the boys brought down their blankets and pillows and asked if they could watch TV. I said yes. They came downstairs and played on the floor in front of the TV with Drake while I made some popcorn."

Buried in the middle is that suddenly her sister left the house after nine or nine-thirty p.m. The kid sister would later claim that since she couldn't reach her boyfriend by phone that she needed to go to his apartment to see him so that he wouldn't be worried about her.

This makes no sense. If he wasn't answering her calls then it's pretty obvious he wasn't worrying about her.

Instead I think what happened was that Darlie accused her husband and her sister of having an affair and she told them both to get the hell out of her house.

Darlie's kid sister would later claim that she was the last person who got to say goodbye to Devon and Damon. She said that the boys were in front of the television and before they went to sleep on the floor in front of the television that she said goodbye to them.

When Darlie's kid sister appeared on the Leeza Gibbons show with Darin and her mother, Darlie Kee, after Darlie Routier was convicted of capital murder and sent to death row, the host asked her what type of mood Darlie was in that evening. And she couldn't answer. Her mother jumped in and answered for her, even though her mother was not the person who was right at the house with Darlie. At commercial break the sister left the stage.

pg. 35 KILLER MOM – DARLIE ROUTIER IS AN OPINION ESSAY ONLY AND IS NOT MEANT TO SERVE AS ANY MEDICAL, LEGAL, OR PSYCHOLOGICAL ADVICE.

So, who is telling the truth? Did the boys camp out in front of the big screen TV before the kid sister raced out of the house? Or did the boys come downstairs AFTER their aunt and their dad suddenly left the house like Darlie said they did?

"About 20 or 25 minutes later Darin came in and sat down with us while we watched TV. Drake started to get fussy so I made him a bottle. Soon after the boys fell asleep. Darin took the baby upstairs and put him in his crib and came back downstairs. We talked about a few problems we were having with the car and the boat and had a few words between us."

Darin did not return in 20 or 25 minutes. At one point after the murders he claimed he was home by ten p.m. However, at another point he claimed that he returned at 10:15.

If he left the house abruptly at nine p.m. and didn't return until 10:15 then where was he? He was with Darlie's kid sister, that's where.

Notice that Darlie admits in her written confession that the two of them "had words". Darin on the other hand never mentioned any trouble between them.

"Since I had the baby I have been having some depression. I told Darin I was depressed because I hadn't been able to take the boys anywhere because we only had one car. He told me he loved me and asked me if I wanted him to sleep downstairs with me because I wanted to stay up a little and watch TV. I told him no because I didn't think he would be able to sleep on the couch and get any sleep."

Darlie admits that since she had the baby she had "been having some depression".

In fact, four weeks before the murders Darlie contemplated suicide and even started writing her suicide note to her children – "Dear Devon, Damon, and Drake – I hope that one day you will forgive me for what I'm about to do…".

Darin would later say that the day Darlie was so depressed that she couldn't drag herself out of bed or stop crying, that they discussed it and he became angry with her for how she was feeling. According to Darin they didn't discuss it again. And just four weeks later two of their children were dead.

"I had been sleeping on the couch the past week or so off and on because the baby slept in our room in the crib and when he moved he woke me up."

Devon and Damon were brutally stabbed within inches of where she claims she was sleeping. And she claims she slept through it all.

"Darin and I laid together for a little while and then decided to go to sleep because he had work the next day, this was around 12:30 or1:00, I'm not sure. He kissed me and said he loved me, and I told him I loved him and would see him in the morning."

Darin says he went to bed at 11:00. Darlie says he went up the stairs to bed without her at 1:00.

And at 2:31 a.m. Darlie says that after she screamed for her husband that she dialed 911.

"After awhile I started to get sleepy. The next thing I wake up and feel a pressure on me. I felt Damon press on my right shoulder and heard him cry, this made me really come awake and realized there was a man standing down at my feet walking away from me."

Darlie's husband owned and carried guns. If there was a stranger in the house, I have no doubt that Darlie would have screamed at the top of her lungs for her husband to shoot him.

"I walked after him and heard glass breaking. I got halfway through the kitchen and turned back around to run and turn on the light, I ran back towards the utility room and realized there was a big white handled knife lying on the floor, it was then that I realized I had blood all over me and I grabbed the knife thinking he was in the garage so I thought he might still be there and I yelled for Darin."

Bull, bull, and more bull from Darlie.

Seriously? If you see a man in your house in the middle of the night, do you really believe that you're going to walk behind him?

Darlie writes as if she picked up the knife to protect herself in case the intruder returned to harm her. Did she lock the garage door behind him? Did she turn on the outside lights?

By the time Darlie claims Darin came running down the stairs the knife was already on the counter. If she honestly picked up that knife to protect herself from an intruder, she would have had that knife in her hand.

"I ran back through the kitchen and realized the entire living area had blood all over everything. I put the knife on the counter and ran into the entrance, turned on a light and started screaming for Darin, I think I screamed twice and he ran out of the bedroom with his jeans on and no glasses and was yelling, what is it, what is it. I remember saying he cut them, he tried to kill me, my neck, he ran down the stairs and into the room where the boys were. I

grabbed the phone and called 911. Darin started giving Devon CPR while I put a towel on my neck and a towel over Damon's back."

According to Darin he had no idea that Darlie was injured. He said later that the only way he learned what had happened was by listening to what Darlie said on the phone to the police dispatcher AFTER she dialed 911. But according to Darlie, she told Darin that she was injured and that both boys had been stabbed BEFORE she dialed 911.

"I remember telling Damon to hang on mommy was there. I looked over at Darin and saw the glass table had been knocked halfway off and the flower arrangement had been knocked over. I then stood up and turned around and saw glass all over the kitchen floor. I tried to glance over to see if anything was out of place or if anything was missing. I took a few steps and opened the door and screamed for Karen. I was still on the phone with 911 and I don't recall what all was said because everything was happening so fast."

Take a closer look at what Darlie just said – "...to see if anything was out of place or if anything was missing." Her children are bleeding to death right before her eyes. But instead of applying pressure to their wounds or holding her children in her arms, she is scanning the house to see if anything was missing.

Also, Darlie claims that while she was on the phone with the police dispatcher that she opened the door and SCREAMED for Karen. This is a lie. Nowhere on the 911 tape is there any evidence that Darlie ever screamed for Karen. (Karen is the neighbor who came to the house while the police were there to take the baby who was found safe and sound in his crib up in the master bedroom).

pg. 39 KILLER MOM – DARLIE ROUTIER IS AN OPINION ESSAY ONLY AND IS NOT MEANT TO SERVE AS ANY MEDICAL, LEGAL, OR PSYCHOLOGICAL ADVICE.

> *"I went back to Damon and by then he had stopped moving and the police walked through the door."*

In fact, the police had already walked through the door just a few minutes after Darlie dialed 911.

> *"The paramedics came and tried to work on the children. Darin was screaming Who Did This Who Did This and I started asking if my babies were dead."*

In fact, before the police officer arrived, Darlie had already told the police dispatcher that Devon and Damon were dead.

> *"Darin was crying and said yes. After that I just remember screaming and showing Darin my neck."*

Again, there is no evidence on Darlie's five-minute and forty-four second phone call with the police dispatcher to show that she was ever screaming.

> *"Darin took me out to the front of the house and by then Darin ran upstairs to make sure the baby was okay and then handed him to Karen our neighbor. I remember them holding a towel on my neck and wrapping my arm and then they put me in an ambulance. Darin got in but they told him he needed to leave so they could take care of me. I remember we got to the hospital and then them telling me they were taking me to surgery. They took off my necklace and put me to sleep. I woke up and minutes later the detectives were there making me all kinds of questions."*

Darlie's supporters insist that her necklace was so deeply imbedded in her neck wound that it had to be surgically removed. Yet, in her own words, Darlie says "They took off my necklace and put me to sleep". Clearly, this shows that the necklace was not imbedded in her neck wound.

I think it's interesting that Darlie says the detectives were there within minutes of her waking up from surgery and making her answer "all kinds of questions".

Does the word "minutes" mean sixty minutes? One hundred minutes? And if your children are dead and you want the police to find the murderer, then do you think you would play victim for being interviewed by the police? Or do you think you would be wanting to speak with the police as soon as possible to help them find the monster who murdered your children?

Overall, I find it very interesting that in Darlie's written police statement she does not mention anything at all about the mysterious black car in the neighborhood that she would later claim she had seen driving by her house. I think it's interesting that she spent so much time writing about incidental details while she and her husband were due to receive friends and relatives at the funeral home. And perhaps most glaring of all, I think it's interesting that Darlie attempts to minimize the difficulties the couple was having. Specifically, I think that Darlie's rage that night stemmed from her husband and her kid sister taking the time off together the afternoon before the murders. And I think that's exactly why her first sentence was what I think was an attempt to ward the investigators off at the pass.

~

Statement of Darin Routier

Taken by Rowlett P.D., June 8, 1996

"We were watching TV in the Roman Room (Living Room SW Corner of House) watching [illegible] movie on HBO (Satellite). Baby Drake had fallen asleep about 10-10:30. I took him up to bed in parents

room. Put blanket on him and turned out lights. I went down stairs to talk to Darlie."

It's interesting that Darin claims the baby fell asleep right when he was reported to have returned from taking his wife's sister to her boyfriend's apartment. I also think it's strange that he refers to his bedroom as the "parents" room. That makes no sense. If you are saying that you took the baby upstairs to your room then that's exactly what you would say. But the "parents" room makes it sound as if Darin is attempting to tell the story from a third-person perspective. That's what people sometimes do when they are trying to stick to their script.

"We talked about the boys not being able to start base-ball yet because we were so busy with the baby right now. We talked about the business, bills, and how Darlie was having a hard time with taking care of the baby's (all) today. Darlie said she wanted to sleep on the couch because she would sleep better because the baby would keep her awake."

Again, based on both Darlie and Darin's statements to the police, one point is clear – Darlie is known to be a light sleeper. How can it be that such a light sleeper was able to sleep through two of her children being murdered just inches away from her and her own throat and arm being cut?

I also find it interesting that Darlie struggled with taking care of the children that day. She had an elderly woman who was paid to be there with her all day long to help her with the housework. Her two older children spent the day outdoors or at a friend's house. She fed the family chicken noodle soup for dinner. And by all accounts the baby was not a fussy baby requiring any extensive care.

"The boys were asleep with pillows and blankets on the floor. Devon was asleep face up in front of TV and Damon was asleep between couch and coffee table by the couch mom was. So I went upstairs to get her a blanket and pillow and came back downstairs to cover her up. We talked a little more about her going to Cancun with some friends across the street and I gave her a kiss goodnight. Told her to dream about me and went upstairs around 1:00am."

I didn't realize that Darin said he went upstairs around 1:00 a.m. Perhaps this detail is one that the case followers have gotten wrong for the last 22 years straight as they insist that Darin said he went to bed at 11:00.

It's interesting that Darin and Darlie both claim they were gushy with each other before he went up to bed without her. Their children are dead after Darlie was raging through her house the day before, slamming cupboard doors and sharpening her kitchen knives, after she learned that her husband and sister had left work and were spending the afternoon together. Then her sister had to leave suddenly at some point between 9:00 and 9:30 even though she had been staying with the family and there was no mention earlier that she would not be spending the night that night too.

Darlie said they "had words between" them. She says they talked about the business and her being depressed. He says they talked about the struggles of taking care of the children all day when the children weren't even home.

And they both insist that their day ended in "I love you" and "dream about me" mush.

I don't believe any of it. I think they fought, and they fought hard. I think the sister went running out the door. And I think when Darin

pg. 43 KILLER MOM – DARLIE ROUTIER IS AN OPINION ESSAY ONLY AND IS NOT MEANT TO SERVE AS ANY MEDICAL, LEGAL, OR PSYCHOLOGICAL ADVICE.

returned to the house that he and Darlie fought some more. I think he told her they were through and went to bed. And then I think he heard his children screaming for his help.

"I went and turned on TV in our room and watched for 10 to 15 min. and took my glasses off and turned TV off. I could not go to sleep for a while but finally I fell asleep. Uncontisly (sic) I heard a noise and then Darlie screaming loud."

Keep in mind that while Darlie and Darin are writing out their statements for the police investigators that they are supposed to be at the funeral home for the one visitation which will take place before they bury their sons the following day.

And they are writing about popcorn, and plates, and blankets, and pillows. I don't believe any of it. When a father who has just lost two of his sons in a savage attack against his family writes about taking his glasses off, I suspect that instead of telling the truth at all that both Darlie and Darin were trying to get, and to keep, their stories straight.

"She was yelling Devon! Devon!! Oh my God Devon! I woke up quickly and grabbed my glasses on the night stand and ran downstairs as fast as I could. Going into the Living Room (Roman) I ran over to Devon laying on the floor where he was when I saw him last and nealed (sic) down over him to see if he was hurt and then looked at the coffee table to see it tipped over on him. When I looked again at his chest there were two holes in his chest with blood and muscle piecing(sic) out.

Sometimes Darin says that he woke up when he heard the soft "swoosh" of a wine glass breaking on the kitchen floor. Sometimes Darin says that he woke up when he heard Darlie screaming out "DARIN, DARIN, DARIN!" But in his written statement to the police, he says that he woke up when he heard Darlie scream out the name of their oldest son.

"I slapped his face to get him to say or look at me. No response. I started CPR and when I blew into his mouth air came out of his chest. I blew 5 or 6 times and held my hand over the holes on his chest. Then when that didn't work I blew into one of the holes in his chest. I looked over at Darlie and she was on the phone calling 911."

Darin's attempt to perform CPR would have taken him fewer than one minute, at the most, since blowing air into the young boy's body resulted in blood spewing out from his chest wounds. So, what exactly was Darin doing the rest of the time? My guess is that he was planting the sock outside about fifty to seventy-five yards away. Keep in mind that when the police officers arrived at the house that the outside security lights were not on. Darlie said the intruder had just walked toward the garage when she screamed then dialed 911.

The first officer arrived just over three minutes later. And the outdoor security lights were not on when he arrived.

So, whoever dropped that sock out in the yard had to have known exactly where the outdoor sensors were located in order to avoid turning the outdoor security lights on considering they were on a timer and once they were activated they stayed on for fifteen minutes straight.

"I ran over to Damon laying on floor in hallway between wall and side of couch. He had no pulse but I could not see any injuries. Police came in and I told them that my babys were stabbed and she told them that he went out of the garage. I ran upstairs to put my pants on. I looked over and Drake was crying and I felt

[illegible] he was ok. I noticed my wallet left on the floor and all I could think to do was to go to Karen's house for help. I needed someone to help [illegible] and [illegible] the paramedics when they arrived. I went downstairs ran out the house and ran across the street to Karen and Terry door. I banged 5-6 times as hard as I could until Terry comes to the door 1st and when I told them that Devon and Damon were stabbed they were in shock and ran over with me to the house and that was when they were putting Damon on a stretcher."

This is all very confusing considering that the first responding officer observed Darin attempting to perform CPR on his older son when the officer entered the house. Other times we hear that when the officer arrived at the scene that Darin was outside in the front yard saying that he was going to go to the neighbor's house to get "Karen" who I think was a nurse.

Darin says that he ran back upstairs to put his jeans on and that he checked on the baby and the baby was "ok".

Remember, Darin was a gun toter. Did he grab his gun when by that time he was told by Darlie there was a monster lurking in their garage who had just stabbed two of their children? No. There is absolutely no mention at all of Darin grabbing one of his firearms either the first time he ran down the stairs or when he supposedly went back up the stairs to put his jeans on.

Did he legally own his guns? Was he legally allowed to carry them? Why is it that such an avid gun owner and toter didn't think of grabbing one of his firearms the first second that he heard his wife scream?

"I knew that Devon was dead before I ran across street and Damon had no pulse, but the paramedic carried him out in a blanket

out the front door. I ran out yelling that we have to find who did this and Karen told me that Darlie was cut too! I never knew that she was hurt yet she had blood all over her from the neck down to the bottom of her nightshirt. She was standing in the door way with the paramedics said she needed to go to the hospital. So we helped her onto the stretcher and she said "Darin you have to promise me we will find this man! He killed our babys."

"I walked back into house pushed my way through the police and saw the knife on the bar in kitchen w/blood all over it. [illegible] went to garage [illegible] to look at the window that the police had said he entered and I went out of the house and walked across the street and neighbors were there to comfort me and ask me about what happened."

What Darin doesn't mention in his written police statement is that when the officers arrived at the scene Darin told them to check out his wife. Specifically, Darin pointed out Darlie's breast implants and said wow, just look at her! Isn't she beautiful?

It's interesting to see that Darin says he "pushed" his way through the police and looked at the knife on the counter and then went out to the garage to see the window that the police said the intruder must have climbed through. Could it be that Darin wanted to be sure to be seen by police in both areas just in case it turned out that it was his prints on the knife or on the window?

"I sat for a minute on a curb and walked over to the ambulance where Damon was and asked paramedic was he alive and they said no. I was in shock. Karen told me to go with Darlie in the ambulance. So I got in and they threw me out and said they needed to work. So then they asked me questions (fire dept) (SS# + address + name) and I asked what hospital and no one knew. So *found out where Darlie went (Baylor Dallas) and drove over to the hospital. At hospital I was questioned by Det. Frosch for hours."*

Darin's children were dead. They were killed just two days before he gave this written statement to the police.

Years later, Darin would sign an affidavit stating that he had been asking around for someone to break-in to his home, so he could make some quick cash from the insurance company. Yet, nowhere in his written statement did Darin mention that the person responsible for his children's murders may have been someone who was taking him up on his offer to be paid to help him stage a break-in. In the ABC miniseries which aired in June of 2018, Darin explained that Darlie's lawyers told him to sign the affidavit if he wanted to help Darlie's chances of successfully appealing her conviction.

While I find it hard to believe that a lawyer would tell a convicted killer's husband to lie in a sworn affidavit, I find it equally troubling to believe that if in fact he was asking around for someone to help him stage a break-in that he wouldn't have included that in his statement to the police.

Overall, I think that both Darlie and Darin were lying from the moment Darlie first dialed 911 and I think they have both been lying ever since. I think that Darlie murdered two of their children and that Darin has been covering for her from the start.

Not because he loved Darlie so much or because he ever believed in her. I think that Darin has been lying for Darlie because I think Darin blames himself for what she did.

~

Here are excerpts taken from one of the many docudramas that have been created specific to Darlie's case.

Announcer - "She led a charmed life. But now Darlie Routier sits on death row for murdering her children, Damon and Devon."

Darlie - "I've been wrongfully convicted. I'm innocent. I've been done wrong!"

Prosecutor Greg Davis - "She is a cold-blooded killer".

Announcer - "Some are wondering, did Darlie do it?"

Reporter - "The woman who sat across from me - either she's an academy award winning actress or she didn't murder those boys".

Darin - "We will not stop until we prove her innocence and she's home".

Darlie - "I am 100% innocent. I did not murder Devon and Damon".

~

~

Darlie - "I've been wrongfully convicted. I'm innocent. Uh, I've been done wrong!"

Darin - "The first thing I hear is this real light glass break - swoosh - the next thing I hear is Darlie screaming, I mean screaming as loud as any person you've ever heard..."

Darlie on the 911 call "My babies are dying! They're dead!"

James Cron (retired investigator called in to help the Rowlett police investigate the murders of Devon and Damon Routier) - "...one of the victims became the suspect. We didn't start looking at the mother until 20 to 30 minutes in when I told them I said something is wrong with this scene".

Rowlett Police Department - "No one is being ruled in or out as suspects".

pg. 49 KILLER MOM – DARLIE ROUTIER IS AN OPINION ESSAY ONLY AND IS NOT MEANT TO SERVE AS ANY MEDICAL, LEGAL, OR PSYCHOLOGICAL ADVICE.

Darin – "What I had was like a utopia compared to what my life is like now".

Announcer – "...the Routiers were young, only in their mid-twenties. But apparently affluent".

Darlie – "I was living, um, what a lot of people can only hope to live. You know I'm very fortunate. I felt very blessed. Um. Had a wonderful happy home. Three little healthy happy boys. Um, good marriage. You know, we were happy".

Announcer – "The family lived in a quarter of a million-dollar home. Had expensive cars. Had a boat on a nearby lake..."

This is an absolute lie. The family lived in a home they quite likely purchased with zero down payment for under one hundred and thirty thousand dollars. At the time of the murders they owed more on the house than it was worth. Expensive cars? The cars owned by the family were not expensive at all. One was not even running at the time of the murders. They were a one-car family which did not even qualify for a five-thousand-dollar loan. The boat? The boat was also "purchased" with zero down payment and at the time of the murders it was broken down and not even in the water.

Then the docudrama skidded completely off the rails by suggesting that poor Darlie was convicted of capital murder all because the jurors were allowed to see the video of the party Darlie held shortly after her sons' murders which show her laughing and spraying silly string on their shared grave.

Please be clear on this point – Darlie was not convicted of capital murder because of any silly video of her spraying silly string on her sons' grave. She was convicted of murder because the evidence at her trial supported the fact that she is guilty beyond any reasonable doubt.

The docudrama then tried to make a big deal out of typos in the court transcript. Again, the docudrama is attempting to deflect the viewers' gaze from the facts of the case in order to promote the absurd rhetoric of her supporters that poor Darlie was wrongfully convicted.

Announcer – "While the fight goes on for Darlie..."

Announcer – "But many troubling questions remain".

The only "troubling question" that I have is why is Darlie allowed to benefit by fundraisers which have been held in her name since her arrest? Isn't there some sort of law in Texas which prohibits a convicted murderer from raking in money based on the notoriety of her case? If not, it seems there should be.

The appeals lawyer who many years later Darin would state in the ABC docudrama told him if he wanted to help Darlie then he would lie in a signed affidavit, states that he is "confident that upon a new trial with some of the information that we now have and a little bit different approach" that Darlie would be found not guilty of capital murder.

Yet twenty-two years have passed, and the defense team has yet to secure a successful appeal.

Prosecutor – "Nothing whatsoever has changed. I mean any person capable of killing a helpless five-year-old child and a six-year-old child in the manner that Darlie Routier killed these two children deserves the death penalty. And those two children deserve a measure of justice too".

Darlie – "I have to keep fighting, because I have to fight for the truth, I have to fight for Devon and Damon, I have to fight for me".

~

pg. 51 KILLER MOM – DARLIE ROUTIER IS AN OPINION ESSAY ONLY AND IS NOT MEANT TO SERVE AS ANY MEDICAL, LEGAL, OR PSYCHOLOGICAL ADVICE.

If Darlie is truly interested in fighting for the truth it just might help if she would begin by speaking the truth of what happened the night she murdered her children.

~

Darlie's trial testimony

Darlie had the very best legal defense team that other people's money could buy. Her lead attorney was Doug Mulder who at the time was known as being one of the very best criminal defense lawyers in the entire state of Texas. Perhaps she should have listened to Mulder's advice when he told her not to take the stand.

Excerpts from Cross-Examination by Prosecutor Toby Shook

5 Q. And, as far as the home goes, you were

6 the one that decided decorating the home, making

7 purchases for the home, how it looked, and that kind of

8 thing, did you not?

9 A. Well, most of it, yes.

10 Q. And you would keep the house up, and

11 keep it clean, and that kind of thing?

12 A. Yeah, I had help.

13 Q. When did you start getting help with

14 the house?

15 A. Well actually, I had had a maid

16 service for quite sometime.

17 Q. When did that start?

18 A. I don't have any exact date for you.

19 I can say, approximately, two years ago.

20 Q. Okay. And, would they come in every

21 week?

22 A. Yes, sir.

23 Q. Okay. And then, of course the week of

24 the murder, you had Babcia come in for a couple of days?

25 A. Yeah, if I can explain. The people 1 that I was having clean, they had changed to a bunch of

2 different people, and they weren't doing as good of a job

3 as what they normally would do. And so, I had let them

4 go, and I had another lady come in and clean, and she was

5 very nice, but every time she cleaned she ended up

6 breaking something. And, it ended up costing me more

7 money to have her clean, than what it was -- what she was

8 breaking.

9 Q. So you were having people then coming

10 in for the last two years helping you clean?

11 A. Yes, sir.

12 Q. You also -- did you have some of these

13 teenage girls help you watch over the kids?

14 A. Well, I wouldn't necessarily say watch

pg. 53 KILLER MOM -- DARLIE ROUTIER IS AN OPINION ESSAY ONLY AND IS NOT MEANT TO SERVE AS ANY MEDICAL, LEGAL, OR PSYCHOLOGICAL ADVICE.

15 over the kids. I think that they -- I think that was

16 kind of an excuse that they used to be in the house.

17 Q. Okay.

18 A. I mean, they didn't really want to say

19 that they were coming over to be with, you know, a five

20 and a six year old.

So, if you're a juror listening to the defendant testify on her own behalf, so far you've learned that she had maids and that she allowed teenage girls to hang out with her at the house. The elderly woman who was at the house the day before the murders testified also. She told the jurors about the time that Darlie held a blanket over the baby's face until he couldn't breathe. She testified that when she finally got the baby away from Darlie that she and one of her young teenage friends went running back up the stairs to Darlie's bedroom as they both laughed at the older woman for being concerned for the baby's safety.

We're not talking about teenagers who were eighteen or nineteen. We're talking about girls who were twelve and thirteen years old who spent their time hanging out with Darlie.

As if they were friends.

Not with her children.

But with her.

~

At Darlie's trial the location of her vacuum cleaner became a big focal point for the prosecution. There was blood found underneath the vacuum cleaner which helped to support the investigators' claim that the crime scene was staged.

2 Q. That is where you keep your vacuum

3 cleaner?

4 A. Usually, yes, sir.

5 Q. Every day? I mean, that is where we

6 would find the vacuum cleaner?

7 A. Well, not every day. Sometimes it

8 would be upstairs. I have two vacuum cleaners.

9 Q. Well, do you have closets in the

10 house?

11 A. Not very many. There's one.

12 Q. One closet in the house?

13 A. One hallway closet, as far as clothes

14 closets, there's a couple.

15 Q. And, so the vacuum cleaners, they

16 don't fit in any of the closets, they have to be out all

17 the time?

18 A. I guess you could try to fit them in

19 there.

20 Q. Well, you keep a pretty neat house,

21 don't you?

pg. 55 KILLER MOM – DARLIE ROUTIER IS AN OPINION ESSAY ONLY AND IS NOT MEANT TO SERVE AS ANY MEDICAL, LEGAL, OR PSYCHOLOGICAL ADVICE.

22 A. To a certain extent, yes, sir.

23 Q. I mean, you are pretty famous for

24 having a very neat house, aren't you?

25 A. I like to keep a neat home.

1 Q. But you don't put your vacuum cleaners

2 away?

3 A. Well, it wasn't like an important

4 thing, that I made sure that I put my vacuum cleaner

5 away.

6 Q. And that night, I guess when you were

7 lying on the couch then, the vacuum cleaner was against

8 the bar over there?

9 A. Yes, sir. I had been vacuuming.

The Routier home was massive. And it was brand new when they bought it a few years before the murders. Do you really believe that the house had just one closet? OH! Wait! She didn't mean the clothes closets. Oh, yeah, sure! The house had two clothes closets. Of course!

If you're sitting on the jury and you see her skirting the issue of putting her vacuum away, what are you going to think about her credibility at this point? You will begin to believe that she is lying.

~

23 What were you about to do?

24 A. I was contemplating suicide.

pg. 56 KILLER MOM – DARLIE ROUTIER IS AN OPINION ESSAY ONLY AND IS NOT MEANT TO SERVE AS ANY MEDICAL, LEGAL, OR PSYCHOLOGICAL ADVICE.

25 Q. Pretty seriously?

1 A. If it would have been seriously, I

2 wouldn't be here today.

3 Q. Well, you are writing a note?

4 A. Yes, sir.

5 Q. "I hope that one day you will forgive

6 me for what I am about to do"?

7 A. Yes, sir.

8 Q. And you have got the pills, I mean,

9 that's the way you were going to do it, right? Take

10 pills?

11 A. That's what I was thinking about.

12 Q. And you were going to the trouble of

13 writing this note?

14 A. Yes, sir.

15 Q. So we're talking about some pretty

16 serious contemplation, aren't we?

17 A. Yes, sir, but you also have to

18 consider that I stopped in the middle of that note and

19 called my husband, because I had decided that I wasn't

20 going to do that, and that it was silly.

21 Q. Now, why were you so desperate, at

22 that point in your life, one month before these murders,

23 that you were thinking about committing suicide?

24 A. I cannot answer that question for you.

25 Q. Do you have amnesia about that?

1 A. No, sir.

2 Q. You don't have traumatic amnesia about

3 why you were so desperate to think about committing

4 suicide?

5 A. No, sir, I don't.

6 Q. But you didn't purchase those pills

7 while were you contemplating it?

8 A. No.

9 Q. Okay. Those had just been lying

10 around the house?

11 A. They had been in a box, in the house.

12 Q. Okay. How long had they been there?

13 A. How long had they been what, in the

14 house?

15 Q. Right.

16 A. For quite sometime.

17 Q. Okay. Do you remember the first time

18 that you met your psychiatrist on the 20th of June, she

pg. 58 KILLER MOM – DARLIE ROUTIER IS AN OPINION ESSAY ONLY AND IS NOT MEANT TO SERVE AS ANY MEDICAL, LEGAL, OR PSYCHOLOGICAL ADVICE.

19 asked you about your thinking about suicide?

20 A. Lisa?

21 Q. Yes.

22 A. I guess so, sir.

23 Q. You don't have any other

24 psychiatrists, do you?

25 A. No, sir.

1 Q. Okay.

2 A. Well, I mean there was different

3 people that talked to me in the jail.

4 Q. Okay. Do you remember telling her

5 that you thought about suicide, actually bought over the

6 counter pills, wrote note, but knew she couldn't, and

7 called husband?

8 A. Yes, sir.

9 Q. Okay. So you told her that you

10 actually bought over the counter pills?

11 A. I had bought over the counter pills.

12 Q. For the purpose of taking them to

13 commit suicide?

14 A. No, sir. I did not buy the pills that

15 day. If that is, I mean, what you are asking. I'm not

16 sure.

17 Q. So you felt bad enough on the 3rd of

18 May, to sit down and contemplate how you would kill

19 yourself, write a note, and then decided to call your

20 husband?

21 A. Yes, sir.

22 Q. I guess you were not very happy with

23 your life at that point?

24 A. Well, I was feeling pretty depressed.

25 Q. Have you ever thought about committing

1 suicide at any other time in your life?

2 A. No, sir.

Notice how Darlie appears to not be able to answer a direct question. Was it a serious attempt? Darlie's response was that if it was, then she wouldn't still be alive.

This is not helping Darlie gain any credibility. In fact, she seems snarky at times during her testimony as if she simply doesn't have a clue that playing games with the prosecutor right in front of the jurors will most certainly not end well for her.

Darlie is on trial for murder. And she's getting hissy toward the prosecutor about how many closets she has, whether she has paid help at home, and now whether she had purchased the over-the-counter pills that day to kill herself or some day previous to the day she says that she "contemplated suicide".

Take another look at what she wrote in her journal – she is hoping that her children will one day be able to forgive her for what she was about to do.

What if what she was about to do wasn't suicide at all? What if one month before the murders when she wrote that note to her children she was actually contemplating their murders?

~

Darlie claims that she was molested by one of her stepfathers. She says the sexual abuse started when she was just eight years old. Yet, she handed her children over to the man who she claims molested when she was a child just a few weeks before she killed her sons.

3 Q. You said that you mentioned on your

4 direct testimony about being molested a little by your

5 --

6 A. Step-father.

7 Q. Step-father. What's his name?

8 A. Denny.

9 Q. Okay. And, that happened when -- how

10 old were you?

11 A. The first time I was eight years old.

12 Q. Okay. And where is he now?

13 A. He lives -- I'm not exactly sure what

14 the name of the place is, but it's a little bit further

15 outside of Terrell, on one of those little tiny,

16 drive-through towns.

17 Q. Okay. When is the last time you saw

18 him?

19 A. The last time I saw him, I believe was

20 on Mother's Day, he came over to pick up Danielle, my

21 little sister.

22 Q. That is Mother's Day of this last

23 year, 1996; right?

24 A. Yes, sir.

25 Q. Which would have been how close to the

1 murder?

2 A. Well, I don't know, about three weeks

3 maybe.

4 Q. Okay. It's in May, right?

5 A. Mother's Day is, yes, sir.

6 Q. Okay. And in fact, on that date, you

7 gave him Damon and Devon, and let them go with him to his

8 home to stay for a couple of days, didn't you?

9 A. For a day.

10 Q. For one day?

11 A. Yes, sir.

12 Q. This is the man that molested you?

13 A. Yes, sir.

14 Q. And you let him have your children?

15 A. Yes, sir. Can I explain that?

16 Q. Just answer my question. I mean, if

17 your lawyer here wants to you explain it, he can have you

18 do that.

19 A. Okay. That is fine.

20 Q. Okay. And how long were they gone?

21 A. A day.

22 Q. Okay. Incidentally, as far as that

23 accusation of the molestation, the police were never

24 called, were they?

25 A. No, sir, I was eight years old.

1 Q. Okay. When did your mother divorce

2 him?

3 A. I think I was about 17 when she got the

5 actual divorce from Denny, it was about four or five

6 years ago.

Darlie's answer makes no sense. Darlie was already 26 or 27 years old when she murdered her children. The trial took place seven months later, so she was either 27 or 28 years old. If her mother just divorced the man who molested her when she was a child "four or five years ago" then she would have been 22-24 years old at the time of the divorce, not 17 as she claimed.

In my opinion, the sexual abuse Darlie says happened when she was a child truly happened and perhaps served as the core to her rage. Remember that she was angry when she learned that her husband and her kid sister were spending the afternoon together. Alone.

Her kid sister was just fifteen or sixteen years old at the time of the murders. Yet, she was not living with her and Darlie's mother and Darlie's stepfather, she was living instead between her sister's house and her boyfriend's apartment.

Why?

Could it be that Darlie's rage was not toward her sister at all but toward her husband if she did, in fact, suspect him of taking advantage of her kid sister?

7 Q. But on that Mother's Day your children

8 were with him?

9 A. Yes, sir, after Mother's Day.

10 Q. Is that your usual practice not to

11 have your children with you on Mother's Day?

12 A. No, they were with me half of the day.

13 Q. Okay. So, that is not your usual

14 practice not to be with your children on Mother's Day?

15 A. No, sir.

I don't understand how it is that a woman who claims that her father or stepfather molested her when she was a child would hand her children over to him. Did she think they were safe because they were boys? Did she think he had somehow changed? Or did she simply not bother to think at all?

~

14 Q. Okay. The Silly String party, as I

15 guess it's come to be known?

16 A. Yes, sir.

17 Q. You are saying that was not your idea?

18 A. No, sir, it was not.

19 Q. Okay. Did you not go around the

20 neighborhood telling all the kids and parents that they

21 needed to come to this party?

22 A. I called everybody, yes, sir, I did.

23 Q. I mean, you did that, didn't you?

24 A. Yes, sir.

25 Q. I mean you were physically walking 1 around the neighborhood going around knocking on doors

2 and telling parents that they needed to bring their kids

3 to the --

4 A. To a couple of their friends' house, I

5 did.

6 Q. Okay. And, this is while the police

7 still had custody of your house; is that right?

8 A. Yes, sir.

9 Q. And, you were walking around the

10 neighborhood, knocking on doors?

11 A. I was not walking around the

12 neighborhood, I went to three homes.

Well, which is it. At first she said she called people to invite them to her party. Then she admitted she went to a "couple" of houses. And then finally she said that she went to three houses.

Keep in mind, according to Darlie, while she was in the neighborhood knocking on doors to invite people to the party she was having at the cemetery there was a killer on the loose.

A killer who she said thought she was dead.

A killer who would have been interested in making sure she wouldn't be able to identify him and send him to death row.

Clearly, if there was a killer on the loose, Darlie would not have been walking around the neighborhood knocking on doors to invite people to her party.

~

13 Q. Okay. And when you -- were you on

14 some type of drugs or something at the Silly String

15 party?

16 A. I had not been taking as much

17 medication as what I was, but yes, I was still on some.

18 Q. Are you trying to blame your behavior,

19 shooting Silly String, laughing and giggling on any

20 medication?

21 A. No, I am not blaming my behavior, I

22 don't think there is anything to blame.

23 Q. Okay. And, the Silly String wasn't

24 your idea, is that right?

25 A. No, sir.

1 Q. But you certainly didn't mind

2 spraying it and things like that, did you?

3 A. I didn't think there was anything

4 wrong with it.

Darlie defended her silly string antics in every interview she ever gave. It was her way of loving her sons. It was done out of pure love for her sons. It was an expression of love.

I don't think anybody had difficulty with a small gathering at the cemetery eight days after the murders to "celebrate" what would have been the older boy's seventh birthday. I think what bothered most people who saw the video was that Darlie appeared to be downright happy. Just eight days after two of her sons were brutally murdered, Darlie had a big smile on her face. She was laughing. And as one juror so eloquently stated after the conviction when she appeared on the Leeza Gibbons show, Darlie was "smackin' her gum".

Darlie was not grieving. She was partying. She was free. Money was rolling in. She was in the spotlight.

And she was even flirting with the young reporter who she and Darin talked with for forty-five minutes straight.

5 Q. And then you saw Joe Munoz out there
6 with a camera?
7 A. Yes, he was.
8 Q. And you talked to him at quite a great
9 length, didn't you?
10 A. Yes, he came over to the grave.
11 Q. You didn't mind talking to him on
12 camera, did you?
13 A. Well, actually in the beginning I
14 didn't want to, but then later on, yes, I did.
15 Q. You warmed up to him pretty quick,
16 didn't you?
17 A. Yes, he is a very nice man.
18 Q. Well, you can kind of tell that from
19 watching the videotape.
20 A. He was very nice.
21 Q. In fact, it's on that videotape, that
22 you say, that this killer, went to your children first,
23 then tried to come to you.
24 A. Yes, sir.
25 Q. But he had to go to them first?
1 A. That's what I said.

2 Q. Okay. Well, were you just imagining

3 that is what happened, and assuming what had happened?

4 A. Well, I think we have all assumed that

5 that is what happened.

6 Q. Okay. So you don't remember that?

7 A. No, sir.

8 Q. You were just making that statement?

9 A. Yes.

10 Q. Because you figured that is probably

11 what happened?

12 A. We all figured that that is what

13 happened.

Notice Darlie's answers while she's testifying under oath right in front of the jurors. She is downright snippy at times. Perhaps her two most obvious incidents of being snippy toward the prosecutors were when she became upset when she realized the prosecutor had access to her mail and then at the end of the trial when the prosecutor was speaking and Darlie, seated at the defense table, angrily blurted out that the prosecutor was a liar.

According to Darlie and Darin it seems that everybody involved in the case is a liar. Except for the two of them, of course. The CPS workers were liars. The police officers were liars. The doctors were liars. The nurses were liars.

Yet, it was Darlie and Darin who failed the lie detector tests. And it was Darlie's own mother who would go on to lie about whether Darlie had even taken a lie detector test in the first place.

~

What is the truth?

Well, I can tell you what isn't true.

It is not true that Darlie was convicted of capital murder because of a silly string video.

It is not true that the police screwed up the crime scene or failed to properly investigate the case.

It is not true that the nurses all got together and decided to lie under oath to make sure that Darlie was found guilty of murdering her children.

It is not true that Darlie almost died from her injuries. In fact, at the crime scene, according to the EMT who treated her, Darlie's blood pressure and pulse rate were both normal. She was standing. She was talking. She was not in the hospital for two days because her life was in danger. She was in the hospital for two days because the doctors were trying to do her a favor by keeping her out of reach of the reporters who were chomping at the bit to get an interview from her.

It is not true that Darlie and Darin had money, a successful business, or a good marriage.

It is not true that Darlie did not have a good lawyer. She had the best criminal defense team in the state of Texas.

It is not true that Darlie was treated unfairly when the judge moved the location of the trial to Kerrville, Texas. In fact, it was Darlie's lawyer who requested the change of venue.

pg. 70 KILLER MOM – DARLIE ROUTIER IS AN OPINION ESSAY ONLY AND IS NOT MEANT TO SERVE AS ANY MEDICAL, LEGAL, OR PSYCHOLOGICAL ADVICE.

It is not true that the police failed to preserve the evidence or to test the evidence from the sofa that Darlie said she was sleeping on while her sons were murdered within inches of her and while she was attacked with a knife slash to her throat and a stab to her arm. In fact, the police investigators did inspect the sofa. And within a short time after releasing the sofa back to the family, they scrubbed it clean and sold it at one of the fundraisers.

~

2 Q. Let's me ask you this, do you think

3 that you slept while that man stabbed your boys?

4 A. I have no idea.

5 Q. Well, do you think you could have

6 slept through that?

7 A. I don't know how to answer that,

8 because I don't know.

9 Q. Well, you are a light sleeper, aren't

10 you?

11 A. I wouldn't necessarily call it a light

12 sleeper.

13 Q. Well, don't you wake up whenever the

14 baby moves in his crib?

15 A. Yes, sir, but that is not exactly a

16 real light noise.

17 Q. So, when your baby rolls over, you

pg. 71 KILLER MOM — DARLIE ROUTIER IS AN OPINION ESSAY ONLY AND IS NOT MEANT TO SERVE AS ANY MEDICAL, LEGAL, OR PSYCHOLOGICAL ADVICE.

18 wake up?

19 A. His crib is on a hardwood floor and it

20 has rollers on it, and when he wiggles and moves, it

21 shakes the whole crib, and it makes, I mean, it's a

22 pretty loud noise.

23 Q. That is why you were sleeping

24 downstairs, right?

25 A. It's one of the reasons, yes.

1 Q. I mean, that is what you put in your

2 voluntary statement, did you not?

3 A. Yes, sir.

4 Q. I mean, no one forced you to write

5 that down, did they?

6 A. No, sir.

7 Q. I mean, this is in your handwriting?

8 A. Yes, sir.

9 Q. Okay. And don't you say, "I had been

10 sleeping on the couch the past week or so off and on

11 because the baby slept in our room, in the crib, and when

12 he moved he woke me up?

13 A. Yes, sir.

14 Q. Okay. So you are a light sleeper,

15 aren't you?

16 A. To some degree.

To some degree? Seriously? If she was sleeping down on the main floor because her sleep was interrupted by the baby moving in his crib then why on earth didn't they move the baby's crib to his own room instead of keeping it in the master bedroom?

I think the prosecutor nailed her with the "light sleeper" questions. She was such a light sleeper that she woke up when her baby moved around. But two of her sons were murdered near her and her throat was slashed and her arm was stabbed and she claims that she may have slept right through it all.

17 Q. And, how close would you say Damon was

18 to you when you went to sleep?

19 A. How close was Damon?

20 Q. Yes, how close was he to you?

21 A. He was very close.

22 Q. I mean within one foot, wasn't he?

23 A. Pretty much so, yes.

24 Q. Easily one foot, lying there right

25 beside you?

1 A. Yes, on the floor.

2 Q. Do you think that you could have slept

3 through a man stabbing him four times in the back?

4 A. Again, I have no idea.

pg. 73 KILLER MOM – DARLIE ROUTIER IS AN OPINION ESSAY ONLY AND IS NOT MEANT TO SERVE AS ANY MEDICAL, LEGAL, OR PSYCHOLOGICAL ADVICE.

5 Q. Well, you know yourself pretty good,

6 do you think you could have slept through that?

7 A. Sir, I cannot answer that. I cannot

8 remember.

9 Q. Do you think you could have slept when

10 this man stabbed your seven year old, Devon?

11 A. I can't answer that question.

12 Q. He was only about four or five feet

13 away from you, wasn't he?

14 A. Yes, he was.

She cannot answer that question? Why not? Does she have any clue how her answers made her look like she was sitting up there trying to play the prosecutor for a fool? Does she have any clue that the jurors were watching as she skirted his questions and feigned ignorance regarding whether common sense would dictate that if she is such a light sleeper that the baby moving in his crib wakes her up then it's obvious she is lying about sleeping through the alleged attacks against her two older children and herself?

15 Q. Well, you are a mother, aren't you?

16 A. Yes, sir, I am.

17 Q. And don't mothers -- aren't they able

18 to tell when their children are in trouble?

19 A. I would like to think so.

20 Q. Aren't they known for being able to

21 hear those noises?

22 A. From an instinct.

23 Q. Have that instinct?

24 A. Yes, sir.

Evidently, Darlie's instincts weren't working on June 6, 1996. And perhaps Darlie actually never did have a mother's instincts considering the fact that she was known to yell at her children to "get the hell out of (her) house".

At one of Devon's birthday parties before his death, Darlie became angry when he accidentally squirted her with water from his new squirt gun. She grabbed him, in front of all of his friends and his friends' parents, and she grabbed a piece of birthday cake and smashed it and smeared it all over his face.

When he started to cry, Darlie told him he deserved it. That does not sound like a mother.

One woman who worked near Darin's shop contacted me and said that Darlie was known to make the children play in the parking lot behind the shop where there was plenty of traffic coming through. I was told that Darlie would tie the baby seat up to the back door and yell at her older sons to keep an eye on the baby while they were expected to play out in the sometimes busy parking lot.

Again, that doesn't sound like a mother and certainly doesn't sound like a woman with motherly instincts.

25 Q. So, don't you think that you would

1 have woken up if a man started stabbing you?

2 A. I have no idea of what happened that

pg. 75 KILLER MOM – DARLIE ROUTIER IS AN OPINION ESSAY ONLY AND IS NOT MEANT TO SERVE AS ANY MEDICAL, LEGAL, OR PSYCHOLOGICAL ADVICE.

3 night.

4 Q. Well, certainly you would have woken

5 up when he started beating you, wouldn't you?

6 A. I have assumed that that is what

7 happened, yes, sir.

8 Q. I mean, you would have to be awake to

9 take a beating like that?

10 A. I would assume so, yes, sir.

11 Q. And, it's your arms that were beaten,

12 weren't they?

13 A. As far as I know, yes, sir.

14 Q. Okay. I mean, you weren't hit in the

15 face, that's for sure, were you?

16 A. Directly in the face?

17 Q. Yes, we can't see any bruises on your

18 face, can we?

19 A. No, sir.

20 Q. Okay. And you weren't stabbed in your

21 face, were you?

22 A. Not stabbed. There were marks on my

23 face.

24 Q. You weren't beaten in the chest,

25 stomach, back or anything like that?

1 A. I have no idea.

2 Q. Well, did you ever see any bruises in
3 your chest, in your back?

4 A. Not bruises, but there was a mark on
5 my breast.

6 Q. But no bruises?

7 A. No bruises.

8 Q. Okay. You didn't complain to the
9 doctors about a big headache, being whacked in the head,
10 or bumps on the head?

11 A. Actually I did complain about feeling
12 pain. I didn't complain specifically in what areas, I
13 was hurting all over from head to toe.

14 Q. Certainly you are not going to wake
15 up -- or you are going to wake up when he cut your
16 throat, aren't you?

17 A. I have no idea, I would assume so.

18 Q. You wouldn't sleep through that, would
19 you?

20 A. I don't know what happened. I would
21 assume so, but I cannot remember.

pg. 77 KILLER MOM — DARLIE ROUTIER IS AN OPINION ESSAY ONLY AND IS NOT MEANT TO SERVE AS ANY MEDICAL, LEGAL, OR PSYCHOLOGICAL ADVICE.

What is with Darlie's refusal to answer a simple question? The answer is obvious. Darlie is playing dumb. She's feigning confusion. She's pretending that she has spotty memories and really has no clue what happened the night she murdered her children.

22 Q. Do you really think that you could

23 have slept when the man cut your throat?

24 A. I don't think so.

25 Q. You couldn't have slept when you got

1 stabbed in the arm either, could you?

2 A. I don't think so.

~

Round and round she goes. She didn't remember anything but she also didn't think that she would have slept through any of it either. Imagine sitting on the jury while she testified. Probably within just minutes of her starting in with her round robin answer games, you would likely be thinking to yourself that Darlie was a liar, through and through.

~

5 Q. If you saw a man attacking your

6 children, you would scream your head off, wouldn't you?

7 A. Yes, sir, unless my mouth was covered.

Unless her mouth was covered? Where on earth did that come from? From the start she has been saying that when she opened her eyes she saw a man "standing" at her feet "walking" away from her. She has never claimed there was more than one intruder. And then suddenly when she is asked if she would scream if she saw a man attacking her

pg. 78 KILLER MOM – DARLIE ROUTIER IS AN OPINION ESSAY ONLY AND IS NOT MEANT TO SERVE AS ANY MEDICAL, LEGAL, OR PSYCHOLOGICAL ADVICE.

children, then her go-to deflective answer is to suggest that maybe the reason she didn't scream is because someone else may have had their hand over her mouth.

8 Q. You would scream for your husband,

9 wouldn't you?

10 A. Unless my mouth was covered, yes, sir.

11 Q. You didn't have any problems screaming

12 for him when he finally got up and came down there, did

13 you?

14 A. My mouth was not covered.

15 Q. Did you find any tape, or any gauze or

16 anything stuffed in your mouth that showed it to be

17 covered?

18 A. No, just except for that it was torn

19 up inside.

20 Q. Okay. It was all torn up inside.

21 A. Well, it felt raw.

22 Q. Did you talk to the doctors about

23 that?

24 A. I talked to the nurse about that, yes,

25 I did.

What? Her mouth was torn up? It felt raw? Seriously? I think that Darlie thinks she really has an answer for everything. But what she doesn't seem to realize is that her answers are showing the jurors that she is a liar.

~

23 Q. And what is the description that you

24 remember, the best description that you have of this man?

25 A. It's not much, he was a taller man,

1 with dark hair.

2 Q. Okay. Let's start with that. How

3 tall was he?

4 A. I cannot give you an exact -- I mean,

5 I can just tell you that he was above -- I would think

6 above six foot.

7 Q. Okay. Above six foot?

8 A. Yes, sir.

9 Q. And I believe you said that he was

10 along Chris Frosch's build; is that right?

11 A. Yes, sir.

12 Q. Are you talking about height-wise?

13 A. Built-wise.

14 Q. Okay. And --

15 A. I mean, I haven't seen Chris Frosch

16 in, you know, I have just seen him in dress clothes, but

17 he seems to be about the same build.

18 Q. Okay. So he is the same height and

19 build as this man that was walking away?

20 A. Well, approximately.

21 Q. Okay. So the man is over six foot,

22 you would say?

23 A. Yes, sir.

24 Q. And he was a white male?

25 A. I don't know that for sure.

She has woken up to a massacre. Her throat is slashed. Her arm is stabbed. And two of her children have been brutally stabbed. She claims that the intruder walked toward the garage and that she walked behind him. She says that when she saw that he dropped the murder weapon on the floor that she picked it up and set it on the counter.

And she can't say for sure whether he was a white male or not?

1 Q. Okay. What kind of hair did he have?

2 A. He had longer hair.

3 Q. How long was it?

4 A. Like here.

5 Q. Okay.

6 A. Whatever you call that.

7 Q. To his collar?

8 A. Yeah.

9 Q. What color was it?

10 A. Well, as far as I could tell, it was

11 dark, because it was dark in there.

This answer makes absolutely no sense. The TV was still on. So, it wasn't "dark in there". But let's play along. Let's just say that it was dark in there, SO DARK that Darlie was not able to see whether the intruder had dark hair or not.

Now let's use some common sense. If it was SO DARK in there that Darlie was not able to see if the intruder had dark hair, then how did she know that he had collar length hair? Surely, if she could see how long his hair was then she would also be able to see what color his hair was too.

~

17 Q. Do you recall talking with a man by

18 the name of Bill Parker, at the Rowlett Police Department

19 on the 18th of June?

(June 18, 1996 was the day that Darlie was finally arrested.)

20 A. Yes, sir.

21 Q. Okay. And, did he show you your

22 voluntary statement?

23 A. No, sir.

24 Q. Did he show you the voluntary

25 statement, and ask you to read over it?

1 A. No, sir.

pg. 82 KILLER MOM – DARLIE ROUTIER IS AN OPINION ESSAY ONLY AND IS NOT MEANT TO SERVE AS ANY MEDICAL, LEGAL, OR PSYCHOLOGICAL ADVICE.

2 Q. Did he ask you, do you want to make
3 any changes in this voluntary statement?
4 A. No, sir. The only thing I saw from
5 him was an arrest warrant affidavit.
6 Q. So you are saying that he never showed
7 you any voluntary statement?
8 A. He did not ever show me my voluntary
9 statement.
10 Q. And, you didn't read over it in front
11 of him?
12 A. No, sir.
13 Q. Okay. And while you talked to him,
14 during that interview, at least six times he accused you
15 of killing your children, and in each response to him,
16 you said "If I did it, I don't remember it"?
17 A. No, sir.
18 Q. You never said that?
19 A. No.
20 Q. Okay. Not once, not twice, not six
21 times?
22 A. I never said that.

I believe the investigator 100% that Darlie said that if she did kill her children she didn't remember it. The investigator has no reason to lie. Just like the nurses, and the doctors, and the CPS workers and every other person involved with the case have no reason to lie. To believe the accusations of Darlie and her family that the entire case was some big conspiracy against her, you would also have to believe that no fewer than thirty professionals got together and decided to risk their careers just to put her away.

Darlie, on the other hand, has been lying since she first dialed 911 at 2:31 a.m. on June 6, 1996 and reported that an intruder had just stabbed her children.

~

6 Q. You knew it was real important to get

7 all this information down, didn't you?

8 A. No, sir, I did not.

What? This is an incredibly simple question. And Darlie failed. Big time. Her children were just murdered. Two days later she is asked by the police investigators for her written statement to help them find the person who murdered her children. And she actually has the gall to pretend that she didn't know that it was important for her to give the officers as much information as possible to help them with their investigation?

Remember her statement to the police – she talked about clearing plates, and changing a diaper, and popping popcorn. Evidently, those details were important to her. Important enough to write out ten pages of details in her statement which made her two hours late for the visitation for her children at the funeral home.

9 Q. You didn't think it was important?

10 A. Not in the way that they are saying

11 it's important.

12 Q. I mean, didn't you think it was pretty

13 important if a detective on the case is asking you to

14 write down what happened that night?

15 A. Sir, at that time, all I was concerned

16 with was getting to the viewing to see my boys.

17 Q. Well, you wrote 10 pages?

18 A. Yes, sir, I did.

19 Q. Okay.

20 A. And that is not -- if you look at that

21 and you compare that to my normal handwriting, you can

22 tell that is pretty sloppy.

23 Q. Okay. We know, that in this voluntary

24 statement, that you never mentioned going to the kitchen

25 sink, do you?

1 A. No, sir, there's a lot of things in

2 there that are not mentioned, I believe.

3 Q. All right. Well, we will get to some

pg. 85 KILLER MOM – DARLIE ROUTIER IS AN OPINION ESSAY ONLY AND IS NOT MEANT TO SERVE AS ANY MEDICAL, LEGAL, OR PSYCHOLOGICAL ADVICE.

4 of those. But as far as going to the kitchen sink,

5 wetting towels, that is never mentioned in here?

6 A. I believe there is mention about

7 getting towels.

8 Q. But wetting towels?

9 A. No, sir.

10 Q. That's not mentioned in there, is it?

11 A. No, sir.

12 Q. Okay. Going to the sink?

13 A. No, sir.

The sink is not mentioned anywhere in

15 here, is it?

16 A. No, sir.

17 Q. Of course at that time, you didn't

18 know that the police had taken your kitchen sink, had

19 you?

20 A. No, sir.

21 Q. You didn't find that out until they

22 released the house back to you?

23 A. Well, actually we were in the house

24 that night, but I didn't even recognize it that night.

25 Q. You didn't recognize the sink gone?

pg. 86 KILLER MOM – DARLIE ROUTIER IS AN OPINION ESSAY ONLY AND IS NOT MEANT TO SERVE AS ANY MEDICAL, LEGAL, OR PSYCHOLOGICAL ADVICE.

1 A. No, sir.

2 Q. Didn't make any mention of the sink

3 being gone?

~

12 Q. Okay. Going to the sink?

13 A. No, sir.

~

Darlie didn't mention going to the sink to wet towels because she didn't go to the sink to wet towels the night she murdered her children. She came up with that little story AFTER she saw that the investigators were inspecting the sink that she stood in front of when she slashed her own throat after fatally stabbing her children.

~

4 Q. Do you remember her asking how could

5 you sleep through your boys being stabbed? How did you

6 sleep through it?

7 A. That is a question I have asked myself

8 many times.

9 Q. Well, do you remember telling her,

10 "Well, I was on sleeping pills that night, Mercedes"?

11 A. No, I don't think I said that.

12 Q. You didn't say that?

pg. 87 KILLER MOM – DARLIE ROUTIER IS AN OPINION ESSAY ONLY AND IS NOT MEANT TO SERVE AS ANY MEDICAL, LEGAL, OR PSYCHOLOGICAL ADVICE.

13 A. No.

14 Q. I mean, you weren't on sleeping pills,

15 were you?

16 A. No, sir, I wasn't.

So, Darlie's friend testified that Darlie said she was on sleeping pills that night. Hmm.

17 Q. Okay. When was it that you started

18 sleeping downstairs on the couch?

19 A. We had slept downstairs on the couch

20 for quite some time. I mean off and on, it wasn't an all

21 the time thing.

Well, this is interesting. Darlie told her friend Mercedes that maybe she slept through being stabbed and her sons being murdered within just inches of where she was sleeping because she was taking sleeping pills that night. And then in court she testified that she didn't take any sleeping pills. So let's add Mercedes to the growing list of people who are either lying, mistaken, or ill-informed.

It's amazing how Darlie and Darin both have the knack for sounding convinced that they are right and everybody else is wrong. This reminds me of Darlie's mother's antics one day outside the courthouse. One of the prosecution team members was being interviewed on camera by the throng of reporters out front. Darlie Kee walked right up to the group and piped right up that what he was saying was A LIE!

His response to her was not acceptable. He called her trailer trash. Not okay. Clearly not okay. But it is also not okay for her to march right up to another person, to call them a liar, and then to feign offense when they insult her right back.

With the way that Darlie acts on the stand I begin to wonder if she has ever been held accountable for anything in her life. Was her trial the first time she was actually expected to answer for her actions? Could it be that Darlie had been getting away with bad behavior for so long in her life up to that point that she honestly believed the jurors would just take her word on it and let her go free?

So when was it that Darlie was lying? Did she lie to Mercedes when she said that she had taken sleeping pills? Or was she lying under oath when she said she did not take sleeping pills that night?

Either way, one point is clear – Darlie was lying.

~

13 Q. Okay. And that dog you had, he barks

14 a lot at strangers, doesn't he?

15 A. He does bark a lot if he is awake.

Oh, my goodness. It looks like Darlie has come up with a good story to tell about why it was exactly that her yappy dog never barked until the police officers entered the house. Good for the prosecutor for not following Darlie right down that rabbit hole where up is down and in is out. By simply asking "If he is awake?" the prosecutor brought it to the jurors attention and moved on.

16 Q. If he is awake?

17 A. Yes, sir.

18 Q. He is not a real old dog, is he?

19 A. No, I believe he is a couple of years.

pg. 89 KILLER MOM – DARLIE ROUTIER IS AN OPINION ESSAY ONLY AND IS NOT MEANT TO SERVE AS ANY MEDICAL, LEGAL, OR PSYCHOLOGICAL ADVICE.

20 Q. Okay. I guess he just slept through

21 this whole thing also?

22 A. No, actually I think when everybody

23 started arriving, he was barking.

Pay close attention to what Darlie said. "I think when everybody started arriving, he was barking." Clearly, if the dog is a barker, then he would have barked at an intruder who entered the house and murdered two innocent children.

~

4 Q. Do you recognize that as a copy

5 of the letter to your friend Karen?

6 A. Yes, sir, that is my handwriting.

7 Q. You say in that letter, and you even

8 underlined it: "Karen, I know who did it, I can't write

9 it down, they read my mail"?

10 A. Yes, sir, at the time I was hoping.

11 Q. You were just hoping?

12 A. Yes.

She was hoping? She didn't say she was hoping. She said I KNOW WHO DID IT. She said she couldn't write it down because they would read her mail. That's absurd! If she knew who did it then obviously the information should have been shared immediately so there was not a killer on the loose.

pg. 90 KILLER MOM – DARLIE ROUTIER IS AN OPINION ESSAY ONLY AND IS NOT MEANT TO SERVE AS ANY MEDICAL, LEGAL, OR PSYCHOLOGICAL ADVICE.

21 Q. Well, we have another letter here to
22 Dear Joe and Terry?
23 A. May I ask you where you are getting
24 all of these letters from, sir?
25 Q. Do you recognize this letter?
1 A. I would like to know where you getting
2 the letters from.
3 Q. Do you recognize this letter?
4 A. Yes, sir.
5 Q. Okay.
6 A. Let me look at it.
7 Q. Okay. First --
8 A. Oh, the jail file in the central room,
9 isn't that illegal?
10 Q. No, it's not.
11 A. It's not? Okay. I thought it was.

Isn't this just priceless that Darlie is upset because the prosecutor has copies of her letters from the jail? She already told her friend Karen in a letter that she couldn't tell her who it was who murdered her sons because the jail reads all of her mail. And then on the stand she said that she thought it was illegal for them to read her mail.

pg. 91 KILLER MOM – DARLIE ROUTIER IS AN OPINION ESSAY ONLY AND IS NOT MEANT TO SERVE AS ANY MEDICAL, LEGAL, OR PSYCHOLOGICAL ADVICE.

This is a clear example of Darlie's twisted truths. She feigns ignorance that her letters would have ever been read when she has already written to her friend that the jail reads her letters.

No wonder the jurors realized she was a liar. Had Darlie listened to her legal team and not testified she would have surely been convicted anyway based on the evidence presented at her trial. But in choosing to take the stand, my hunch is that it made the jurors' job easy.

Her supporters say that poor Darlie was convicted because the jurors simply didn't like her. They claim that the prosecutors were assassinating her character.

What her supporters fail to realize is that Darlie got up on that stand and committed suicide of her character all by herself.

~

14 Q. You are just lying to your relatives?

15 A. I'm not lying to my relatives. That

16 was told to me.

17 Q. Okay. Here is another letter to your

18 Aunt Sherry and family; do you recognize that?

19 A. Yes, sir, I do.

20 Q. Okay. And in this letter, don't you

21 say, "I know who did it, and it's driving me crazy that

22 he is out there running free. What really makes me angry

23 is that I gave the Rowlett PD his name in the beginning

24 and I assumed they would check him out, but they never

25 did. Now he has had time to make up a story, but I

1 believe if he has lot a of pressure he will break"?

2 A. Sir, the man that did this, is out

3 there running free.

4 Q. Did you write that?

5 A. Yes, I did.

6 Q. That is supposed to be Glenn Mize,

7 isn't it?

8 A. Well, either Glenn Mize or Gary.

9 Q. Well, you say in this letter that you

10 gave his name to the Rowlett Police Department and you

11 have already testified that the one name you gave was

12 Glenn's; is that right?

13 A. Yes, sir.

14 Q. So you are talking about Glenn Mize in

15 this letter, aren't you?

16 A. Yes, I think so, yes, sir.

17 Q. You say, "I know who did it."

18 A. Yes, sir.

There is an interesting point to make about "Aunt Sandy". She took notes each day in court and met with family members and friends in the evenings to tell them what had happened that day in court. The witnesses were not allowed to be in the courtroom and hear what the other witnesses said so their testimony would not be influenced in any way by the other witnesses' testimony. Yet, Aunt Sandy thought nothing at all of clearly violating the rules of the court.

And the defense witnesses evidently thought there was nothing wrong with it either as they lined up to hear exactly what other people were saying.

So, while Darlie's supporters like to run around accusing all of the other witnesses of gathering up at the hotel to plan out exactly what they were going to say when they testified, in fact, it was the defense witnesses who were doing exactly that.

~

Prosecutor Greg Davis cross-examining Darin Routier

18 Q. One last subject I want to discuss

19 with you here. That is the fact that you and your wife

20 both have a financial interest in this case, don't you?

21 A. What do you mean?

22 Q. Book deals?

23 A. We haven't made any deals at all.

24 Q. Do you remember back on December 3rd

25 of '96 that you discussed those book deals with Corrine

1 Wells?

2 A. I said that is how we're going to pay

3 for these attorneys, but we're just hopeful thinking.

4 Q. Well, you didn't mention attorneys
5 back then. Didn't you say that you had been approached
6 by 17 to 19 book companies?
7 A. No, sir, that is not true.
8 Q. And do you remember that when you said
9 that to Corrine Wells that you said that you weren't
10 going to settle for the small dollars like 30 or 40
11 thousand dollars? Do you remember that?
12 A. No, sir, I did not say that.
13 Q. Do you remember telling Corrine Wells
14 that, in fact, the defendant was going to write the book
15 herself?
16 A. I don't remember saying that either.
17 Q. And do you remember the reason why she
18 was going to write the book herself, because she was
19 going to cut out the middle man, and that you and she
20 were going to go for the big figures?
21 A. No, sir, I did not say that.
22 Q. That is what you told her back in
23 December, wasn't it?
24 A. No, sir, I did not. There's six
25 people in here writing books right now.

1 Q. I'm just talking about the one --

2 about the one the defendant is going to write?

3 A. I don't know if that is true.

4 Q. You don't know whether she is going to

5 write a book or not?

6 A. I don't know if she is or not.

7 Q. Going to go for the big figures,

8 correct?

9 A. No, sir.

10

11 MR. GREG DAVIS: Pass the witness.

The woman who called me in May of 2016 to tell me that Darlie had admitted to her, face to face, that she did, in fact, murder her children, also told me that Darin told her she better not say a word about what Darlie had said. According to the woman who called me, Darin intended on making big money on both book and movie deals. However, as far as I know, in the last twenty-two years he has not made any money doing either a book or a movie on his wife's case.

~

However, the fundraisers are another story.

On the day of the murders, Darlie's mother launched the very first fundraiser related to her daughter's case. The first fundraiser was to raise money for the boys' final expenses. The grandparents had plenty of money to cover the costs associated with their grandsons' final expenses. Plus, Darlie and Darin had a ten-thousand-dollar life insurance police on the boys too. But the fundraiser was started anyway within just hours of the boys being declared dead.

When Darlie was arrested Darin was late on his shop rent, business was already slow, and the house payment was late. But then the money started flowing in. One of their biggest donors was a successful local businessman who gave the couple tens of thousands of dollars to help them. Then Darin showed up at his house one day uninvited. Darin hopped over the gate and walked right up to the front door. When the reluctant couple went ahead and invited Darin in, he showed them his 1911 that he routinely carried on his person.

When Darin made a rude comment in reference to either his wife's breasts or his wealthy donor's wife's breasts, his donor showed him the door.

It's unclear just how many tens of thousands of dollars that Darlie received from the wealthy couple. But before long, Darlie and Darin were asked to pass lie detector tests before they couple would donate any more money to her cause.

Needless to say, the wealthy couple stopped giving Darlie and Darin any money.

But the fundraisers continued right on without him. For twenty-two years straight.

One of their early efforts to take money from well-meaning people who fell for their stories about poor Darlie being a wonderful mother who would have never harmed her children, was to hold a rally right at the jail where Darlie was locked up pending trial. But when people who lived in Rowlett heard about the upcoming fundraising event planned for Darlie, they became angry. I was contacted by a woman who worked near Darin's shop. She told me that the people in town who had no

pg. 97 KILLER MOM – DARLIE ROUTIER IS AN OPINION ESSAY ONLY AND IS NOT MEANT TO SERVE AS ANY MEDICAL, LEGAL, OR PSYCHOLOGICAL ADVICE.

doubt that Darlie was guilty as sin held a rally of their own the very same day that Darlie's big fundraiser was planned in front of the jail. She said that their rally was huge while just a handful of people showed up to support Darlie Routier.

So, it appears the family struggled at first to get a good fundraising schema going. But once Facebook became popular, their fundraising troubles were over. Year after year, there seems to be another fundraiser launched. And they all pretty much sound the same – All we need is money to test (insert latest assertion) and we will prove that Darlie is innocent!

Sometimes they ask for fifty-thousand dollars. Sometimes they ask for thirty-thousand dollars. Sometimes they say if you can't afford to send very much money then please send money to Darlie's commissary account at the prison so she can buy stamps and letters, and mascara, no doubt.

There is one couple who have shown absolute class throughout this entire ordeal. They are Darin's parents, Sarilda and Len Routier. They have stayed out of the limelight. They've removed themselves from the public stage and devoted their time and energy on raising their grandson, Drake.

Fortunately for Drake, CPS and the court did place him with his paternal grandparents when his mother murdered his brothers. And hopefully for Drake's sake, his paternal grandparents have not raised him with the belief that law enforcement and the courts cannot be trusted.

Because they can be trusted in his mother's case.

~

I don't believe in the death penalty. Therefore, I do not believe that Darlie Routier should be executed no matter how horrible her crimes were. However, I do believe that the state of Texas has the right to decide whether they believe in the death penalty or not. And they do.

So, I have a question. If Darlie Routier was a man, would she still be sitting on death row over two decades after her conviction or would she have been executed long ago?

According to www.chron.com – "Roughly 13 percent (30 of 238) of the inmates awaiting execution in the Lone Star State have been on death row for 25 years or more. That length of stay is nearly a decade above the national average time awaiting execution of 15 years and nine months."

Darlie is nearing the 25-year mark that the "chron" article says will put her in the 13% minority of death-row inmates who are waiting to be executed.

In my opinion, if Darlie Routier was a man, she would have been executed long ago.

~

In my opinion, if Darlie Routier would be honest about her actions the night she murdered her sons, then she would gain a ton of support from people like me who do not believe in the death penalty.

I also think that her husband should fess up to all he knows. And I think that her kid sister should also speak up about what she witnessed just hours before the murders specific to the dynamics of the relationship between Darlie and her husband.

~

Did Darlie have post-partum depression?

pg. 99 KILLER MOM – DARLIE ROUTIER IS AN OPINION ESSAY ONLY AND IS NOT MEANT TO SERVE AS ANY MEDICAL, LEGAL, OR PSYCHOLOGICAL ADVICE.

I don't think so. I think that Darlie had unresolved rage issues stemming from being molested as a child. Three weeks before the murders she handed her children over to spend the day with the man she claims molested her when she was a child.

What did her mother do in reaction to the abuse? Did her mother even know about it while it was happening?

Did Darlie's family expect her to forgive the sinner but not his sins? Did she bottle up her rage toward the man who molested her and then suddenly in a fit of anger did she unleash her rage onto her children?

~

Here are excerpts from the story on Darlie's case with Sylvia Chase on 20/20.

Sylvia Chase - It's a case that refuses to die. Three years after her conviction, Darlie Routier is the talk of Texas.

Prosecutor – There is nothing new.

Supporters – New evidence of her innocence is piling up.

Juror – I don't know who did it, but Darlie Routier didn't do it.

This juror claims that he did not see all of the photos of Darlie's injuries during the trial. However, the other jurors claim they did see the photos in question.

~

Excerpts from Darlie's first prison interview with Sylvia Chase

Prosecutor Greg Davis - The evidence pointed in one direction and one direction only – Darlie Routier.

Just eight days after her children were brutally murdered, Darlie had a party at the cemetery and was videotaped spraying silly string on her sons' shared grave.

Prosecutor – I was in disbelief.

Darlie – If you knew Devon and Damon then you would know that they're up in heaven and they're up there having the biggest birthday party that we could ever imagine.

~

Officer Waddell – He's got his eyes open (Damon). And he's trying to breathe. I told her that she needed to help him but she just wouldn't help him.

Darlie - That's a lie. There's no other word to use. That's a lie.

~

Sylvia Chase – The prosecutor says here is a woman who was depressed, gained weight, post-partum depression, behind in the mortgage, financially strapped.

Darlie – I was a normal person just like anybody else, a normal mother, that has normal, you know, just normal like everybody else, doesn't go to sleep, and all of a sudden just snapped and become a psychotic maniac killer.

Detective Bill Parker - She's as cold-blooded as any person I have ever talked to and I've spoke to a lot of cold-blooded people.

Detective Bill Parker (describing Darlie) - Psychopathic person with absolutely no shame, no guilt, no remorse, no human compassion.

pg. 101 KILLER MOM – DARLIE ROUTIER IS AN OPINION ESSAY ONLY AND IS NOT MEANT TO SERVE AS ANY MEDICAL, LEGAL, OR PSYCHOLOGICAL ADVICE.

Darlie – If I had done this to my children I would be the first person to stand up and say Oh my God I need help. What have I done? You know. A mother couldn't live with herself.

Sylvia Chase – But now Darlie they're saying that you could live it because you're a psychopath and you could kill and then not have a conscience about it.

Darlie – Sure that fits their theory.

Prosecutor – She did everything to herself. She put herself on death row because of what she did to those two children.

James Cron – There were so many inconsistencies that everything she said that occurred that night does not fit anything at the scene. I mean, could it be any worse?

~

Excerpts from Prosecutor Greg Davis during the closing argument in the Guilt or Innocence Phase of the Trial

19 MR. GREG DAVIS: Thank you, Judge.

20 Well, I told you what a guilty woman

21 does and very quickly, as we walk through here, let's

22 talk about what an innocent woman does and doesn't do.

23 You ask yourselves these questions, as

24 I go through here, using the common sense test, and

25 really that is your best thing to hang on to. You have

1 heard a lot, hang on to your common sense. But as I go

2 through here very quickly,

3 Does an innocent woman, a light

4 sleeping innocent woman, does she sleep through the

5 stabbing of a child that is five feet away from her?

6 No, she doesn't.

7 Does an innocent woman sleep through

8 the stabbing of her child as he is one foot away from

9 her?

10 No, she doesn't.

11 What do innocent women do? They come

12 to the defense of their children, is what they do.

13 And does an innocent woman then sleep

14 through her own attack. Puncture wound to the arm,

15 slashes to the neck, stab to the left shoulder. Does an

16 innocent woman sleep through her own attack?

17 You know, I don't even have to answer

18 that one. Your common sense gives you the answer.

19 Absolutely not.

20 But in all three cases, this is what

21 this woman claims to have done, and she did it because

22 she is not an innocent woman.

23 When she wakes up, does an innocent

24 woman look up and see an intruder and not immediately
25 yell upstairs for her husband? No.
1 And does an innocent woman wake up,
2 see her children here bleeding, and then leave them and
3 chase into a darkened kitchen and utility room, after an
4 armed intruder? No.
5 But that is not what this woman did;
6 is it? What she did is not consistent with what an
7 innocent woman does. And, does an innocent woman, while
8 her children are literally bleeding at her feet, look
9 around the room, and make sure that none of her jewelry
10 is gone?
11 Heaven help us if that is what
12 innocent women and mothers do, and that is what parents
13 do. No. They don't do it, but that is exactly what she
14 did that morning. Looking around to make sure the
15 goodies aren't gone from that kitchen bar.
16 And do innocent women, innocent
17 mothers, again, as their children are bleeding, do they
18 worry about leaving fingerprints on a knife handle? Of
19 course not. But that is exactly what this woman did
20 because she is not an innocent woman.

pg. 104 KILLER MOM – DARLIE ROUTIER IS AN OPINION ESSAY ONLY AND IS NOT MEANT TO SERVE AS ANY MEDICAL, LEGAL, OR PSYCHOLOGICAL ADVICE.

21 And do innocent women have to give

22 eight accounts of what happened? All different accounts?

Prosecutor Greg Davis is on a roll. He and Prosecutor Toby Shook were both very impressive with their questioning of the witnesses during the trial. They both seem to be articulate, intelligent, and basically on the ball as they worked to present the evidence against Darlie Routier. But the best part, in my opinion, is this closing argument during the Guilt or Innocence phase of the trial.

23 I'm not going to run through all of

24 them. But basically, to Waddell, the fight was at the

25 kitchen bar. To Walling, the fight was at the couch. To

1 Jody Cotner, Damon shook her and woke her up and followed

2 her in the kitchen.

3 To Dianne Hollon, there is an intruder

4 over her immediately, and she felt pressure and there is

5 a fight at the couch.

6 To Paige Campbell, the intruder is

7 over her, and he tried to stab her. She grabbed at the

8 knife. She never saw his face.

9 To Denise Faulk, Damon was crying to

10 wake her. Struggle at the neck. Wrestling on the couch.

11 Barbara Jovell, Damon woke her by

12 saying "Mommy, Mommy," and pressure on the legs. And in

13 her voluntary statement she just says a man is walking

14 away from her.

15 Listen, folks, if you are telling the

16 truth it doesn't take eight shots at it to get it.

17 Because the truth never changes. Once is enough. But

18 that is not what this woman did, because this woman right

19 here is not an innocent woman. This woman here is guilty

20 of capital murder.

21 And does an innocent woman, can you

22 imagine, in your wildest nightmares, an innocent mother

23 sitting across the table from Bill Parker, and having

24 Bill Parker accuse her of killing her own flesh and blood

25 several times, and remaining polite for a three hour

1 period.

2 Or never denying the fact that she

3 killed her children, and can you imagine an innocent

4 mother sitting across the table from Bill Parker and he

5 says, "I know you killed your children." And an innocent

6 mother just saying: "Hum." (Shrugging shoulders.)

7 No, they don't. That is not what she

8 did, you see, because this woman right here is not an

9 innocent woman. Guilty of capital murder, Darlie

10 Routier.

11 You know you have got a very simple
12 choice here. You have got a choice of either this woman
13 sitting over here, Darlie Lynn Routier, killed her two
14 children, or some mysterious, lucky intruder did it. And
15 he, indeed, has to be a lucky intruder, doesn't he?
16 Happened to pick the night that the
17 window is open. Happens to pick the night where a sock
18 is left conveniently in a utility room. We haven't even
19 mentioned how he got in.
20 I guess the guy just had to slip down
21 the chimney, to get the knife, then go out and then cut
22 the screen, and then come through the utility room. But
23 when he got in there, lucky fellow, the knife is in the
24 butcher block. Lucky fellow that he kills two children
25 without the mother waking. Lucky fellow that when he
1 cuts this woman over here, she can't describe him.
2 Lucky fellow that he drops a knife on
3 the floor as he leaves, arming his victim, and she
4 doesn't pick it up and wound him. Lucky fellow that he
5 leaves no trace in the garage. Lucky fellow that he
6 leaves no trace in the backyard as he leaves.
7 Those are your choices here. And as

pg. 107 KILLER MOM – DARLIE ROUTIER IS AN OPINION ESSAY ONLY AND IS NOT MEANT TO SERVE AS ANY MEDICAL, LEGAL, OR PSYCHOLOGICAL ADVICE.

8 you go through here, and as you look at the hard,
9 scientific, physical evidence, as Mr. Mosty asked you to,
10 and I will also. When you look at that screen being cut
11 by that knife inside the house, as it was, that is really
12 as far as you have to go with the hard, scientific stuff.
13 Because, if that fact is true, that that screen on that
14 window was cut with a knife inside of that kitchen of the
15 defendant, that answers all of the questions that you
16 have in this case right here that you need to answer.
17 Now you know from the scientific
18 evidence that was the case. And as you look at Devon's
19 blood on the back of that T-shirt, you know how that was
20 deposited. And as you look at the boys' blood on the
21 front of the T-shirt, you know how that was transported
22 to her T-shirt.
23 As you look at that utility room
24 floor, you know that the floor is totally inconsistent
25 with the story that she gave. There is no cast off
1 pattern, and you know from the scientific evidence that
2 that was the case
3 The blood on the vacuum, the roll
4 marks that she made in the kitchen as she staged that

5 scene. And the sink being cleaned with the blood hidden
6 behind the closed drawers and doors to that sink.
7 The physical evidence is there. It
8 points not at many people, not at some people, but it
9 points very clearly to this woman right here, Darlie Lynn
10 Routier. And only Darlie Lynn Routier.
11 You know she did it, and they keep
12 saying that I didn't show you why they did it, and I
13 think I did. We have got a pretty good snapshot look at
14 what this woman's life was like back then.
15 It's so desperate that on May 3rd of
16 1996, in this beautifully normal American home, with no
17 problems in it, this woman is contemplating suicide. You
18 know it wasn't good in there. You know the pressures
19 were building up with the children. You know she was
20 unhappy that she hadn't had a girl. She was unhappy with
21 her weight and with her appearance. She is unhappy that
22 she is not getting the attention from her husband that
23 she wants to get out there, and she is unhappy about that
24 financial situation.
25 Those numbers don't lie there. You
1 can see that if you average it out these people are going

2 to take in ninety thousand dollars less than they took in
3 in '95.
4 That is not bad money but when you are
5 used to 260, 170 is not going to cut it. You know the
6 pressure was there. You know why she did it. You have a
7 very good idea.
8 Only God and she knows exactly why she
9 did it. But we have a pretty darn good idea, don't we,
10 of the kind of pressure that was building up that night
11 on June 6th of 1996.
12 You know, these two children here,
13 well, they lived in Rowlett and I never had the pleasure
14 of meeting them, but you know, once upon a time they were
15 ours too. They weren't just Darlie Routier's children,
16 they were ours.
17 You see, they were our neighborhood
18 kids too. The kids we saw running up and down the
19 streets on their bicycles. They were our classmates.
20 They were our students. These children right here.
21 In a real sense they were our future.
22 You know, and as these two precious children, laid on
23 that carpet, looking up with those opened eyes, literally

24 drowning in their own blood as they laid on that carpet,

25 as Mr. Shook said to you, the very last thing that each

1 of these two children saw was their killer.

2 Can you imagine what it must have been

3 like for those two children that morning as they saw this

4 woman right here?

This is the point that Darlie convicts herself of capital murder right in front of the jurors' eyes. The prosecutor is an excellent speaker. He is delivering an excellent closing statement. Instead of sitting quietly at the defense table during the prosecutor's closing statement, Darlie makes the fatal mistake of hollering out that the prosecutor is a liar.

5 THE DEFENDANT: Liar, liar.

6 MR. GREG DAVIS: She says liar now --

7 THE DEFENDANT: You are a liar.

8 MR. GREG DAVIS: See. See. But --

9 THE DEFENDANT: I did not kill my

10 kids.

11 MR. GREG DAVIS: But they looked up

12 there, and they saw this woman right here, in a rage,

13 coming down on them with that knife, and that is the very

14 last thing that they saw. They saw their killer, and

15 after these four weeks, you have seen her too. Her name

16 is Darlie Lynn Routier. She sits here before you. And

pg. 111 KILLER MOM — DARLIE ROUTIER IS AN OPINION ESSAY ONLY AND IS NOT MEANT TO SERVE AS ANY MEDICAL, LEGAL, OR PSYCHOLOGICAL ADVICE.

17 I'll ask you now to go back to that commitment that you

18 all gave to us.

19 You said that if we proved our case

20 beyond a reasonable doubt, as we have in this case, that

21 not only could you, but you would, find this woman guilty

22 of capital murder, and that is exactly what I am going to

23 ask you to do at this time, because the facts in this

24 case show her to be guilty of capital murder.

Darlie's outburst did not serve her well. She was angry and out of control in a court of law. And her timing could not have been worse. Because within just seconds of her angry outburst, her jurors were set to begin deliberations.

~

Excerpts from the ABC miniseries preview which aired in June of 2018.

It was a case that both captivated and horrified the nation.

Darlie - I was in shock. I was completely blindsided. I couldn't even grasp what they were telling me.

Legal consultant – I know that she shouldn't have been proven guilty beyond a reasonable doubt.

Darin Routier – All I know is that Darlie is 100% innocent. The truth is always gonna be there. It's still there now.

Darlie Router – I just remember feeling like these people are wrongfully trying to accuse me of murdering my children and trying to kill me. I remember just feeling so scared. It couldn't be happening. This just couldn't be happening.

pg. 112 KILLER MOM – DARLIE ROUTIER IS AN OPINION ESSAY ONLY AND IS NOT MEANT TO SERVE AS ANY MEDICAL, LEGAL, OR PSYCHOLOGICAL ADVICE.

Prosecutor (about the expert) – What he testified to was that it was cast off blood, that it was consistent with Darlie Routier actually taking the murder weapon, striking the boys, and small bits of blood actually came off the blade and landed on the shoulder area.

Reporter – Greg Davis plays the video (the silly string video) for the jury and he says here's a woman who just lost her children and she's literally dancing on their graves.

Reporter – All twelve jurors raised their hand when asked by the judge if she should get the death penalty for murdering her son.

Darlie Routier – I loved being a mother. I loved Devon and Damon. The idea that I would want to murder my children is just so ridiculous.

Consultant is asked if there's any chance Darlie's conviction will be overturned to which she responds – Absolutely! Um, first and foremost, uh, the state used blood splatter analysis, um, to convict her, and what we've learned in the twenty years since her trial is that blood splatter analysis is highly subjective.

It's interesting that the consultant clearly refers to blood spatter analysis as "blood splatter analysis".

It's also interesting that the consultants for the miniseries are with the innocence project.

Just like the MaM consultants were too.

~

The Darlie Routier case on Facebook

Compared to many of the other high profile cases in the news, the Darlie Routier case discussion groups are relatively civil and offer an excellent opportunity for folks to discuss the case without any of the drama that Facebook is becoming famous for.

pg. 113 KILLER MOM – DARLIE ROUTIER IS AN OPINION ESSAY ONLY AND IS NOT MEANT TO SERVE AS ANY MEDICAL, LEGAL, OR PSYCHOLOGICAL ADVICE.

I started the Darlie Routier Case Discussion group about four years ago and in that time it has grown to roughly 1000 members. Discussion is civil. We have about a seventy / thirty split of members who believe that Darlie is guilty. However, all opinions and comments are welcome as long as members are discussing the case and not each other.

If you're interested in learning more about the case, feel free to join our discussion group. We have a full library of resource materials such as court transcripts, police statements, etc. and we welcome the opportunity to discuss the case with people regardless of whether or not they believe Darlie is guilty.

In closing, I'd just like to remind you that KILLER MOM – DARLIE ROUTIER IS AN OPINION ESSAY ONLY AND IS NOT MEANT TO SERVE AS ANY MEDICAL, LEGAL, OR PSYCHOLOGICAL ADVICE.

Also, the theories and opinions expressed in this essay are the authors alone on very public case with actors who have placed themselves on a very public stage. The author has no intent to hurt anybody's feelings or to unfairly present the facts of the case in such a way that it may be stressful for the friends or family members of the convicted killer mom to read. However, if you are a friend or family member of the convicted killer mom then it just makes sense that you would not be reading this essay in the first place.

About the Author

Brenda Irish Heintzelman, BA, JD is an avid writer and speaker on the issues of family violence and child abuse. Brenda is the owner of mimediator.com and serves as a mediator and arbitrator specializing in domestic relations including custody, access, and child protection.

If you enjoyed this essay on the case of accused killer Christopher Watts please check out Brenda's other true-crime essays which are available on both kindle and amazon.com.

Unbelievable (Darlie Routier)

Confession (Darlie Routier)

The Whole Truth (Darlie Routier)

Haters (Christopher Watts)

Haters (Steven Avery)

Scapegoat (Terri Horman)

The Lie (Colleen McKernon)

Above the Law (Curtis Reeves)

Sacred Bond (Sabrina Limon)

Permission to Scream (Betty Broderick)

Scapegoat (Jodi Arias)

Scapegoat (Mary Winkler)

May 19, 1983 (Diane Downs)

Presumed Guilty (Christopher Watts)

Killer Women

Preview of

PERMISSION TO SCREAM

The Psychosocial Abuse of Convicted Husband Killer Betty Broderick

copyrighted material 2018

Brenda Irish Heintzelman

Early in the morning on November 5, 1989 Betty Broderick shot and killed her abusive ex-husband, Daniel Broderick, III. She didn't intend to hurt him. She intended to kill herself right in front of him if he refused to listen to her final plea to just leave her the hell alone.

He was a powerful well-connected lawyer who tortured Betty long after their separation with incessant court filings claiming she was mentally unstable. He wouldn't let up. And Betty couldn't take it anymore. If he refused to listen to her then her only escape was to commit suicide.

When Betty had taken just two steps into his bedroom he saw her and lunged for the phone. His sudden movement scared Betty and before she knew what was happening "the gun just went off".

Five times.

Betty Broderick was a battered woman long before the syndrome became widely known. She was beaten down for nearly twenty years straight as her husband physically, sexually, emotionally, spiritually, financially, and psychologically abused her.

Betty was stuck in the freeze response survival instinct. She didn't know how to protect and defend herself from his abuse. And in 1989 she didn't have any help.

pg. 117 KILLER MOM – DARLIE ROUTIER IS AN OPINION ESSAY ONLY AND IS NOT MEANT TO SERVE AS ANY MEDICAL, LEGAL, OR PSYCHOLOGICAL ADVICE.

He robbed Betty of all she held dear – her children, her home, her reputation for being a good mother, her marriage, her fair share of the marital assets, and even her china and linens too.

In front of their children he called Betty a "monster" and "the beast".

While feigning concern for his safety, he taunted Betty then acted shocked when she reacted in anger.

He told people she was crazy and would soon take her own life.

He continued to push and prod Betty until finally she decided to give him what he wanted ~ her life.

But then just seconds before she planned to pull the trigger,

suddenly the gun was pointed at her abuser,

instead of herself.

Because sometimes,

battered women fight back.

~

Printed in Great Britain
by Amazon